Cambridge Hidden Walks

Maggie Hartley, Ruth Meyer, Steve Robertson, Sophie Smiley, Chris Weeds and Cathy Willis

Published by Geographers'
A-Z Map Company Limited
An imprint of HarperCollins *Publishers*
Westerhill Road
Bishopbriggs
Glasgow
G64 2QT

HarperCollins *Publishers*
Macken House, 39/40 Mayor Street Upper,
Dublin 1, D01 C9W8, Ireland

www.az.co.uk
a-z.maps@harpercollins.co.uk

1st edition 2023

Text and routes © Maggie Hartley, Ruth Meyer, Steve Robertson, Sophie
Smiley, Chris Weeds and Cathy Willis
Mapping © Collins Bartholomew Ltd 2023

The Publisher would like to thank The Master and Fellows of St John's
College Cambridge for granting permission to direct Walk 6 across land
belonging to the College.

This product uses map data licenced from Ordnance Survey© Crown
copyright and database rights 2022 OS 100018598

A catalogue record for this book
is available from the British Library.

ISBN 978-0-00-856497-1

10 9 8 7 6 5 4 3 2 1

Printed in India

	MIX
	Paper | Supporting responsible forestry
FSC www.fsc.org	FSC™ C007454

This book is produced from independently certified FSC™ paper
to ensure responsible forest management.

For more information visit: www.harpercollins.co.uk/green

contents

introduction

Throughout most of Cambridge's long history, fenland lay between the settlement and the East Anglian coast – dangerous, marshy land, navigable only by boat. Cambridge, on the edge of the fens, became an inland port and thriving market town.

The city is now mainly renowned as home to the world-leading university which dates from 1209, when scholars from Oxford found refuge here. Colleges and other developments followed over the centuries. Perhaps unsurprisingly, although the city has now expanded widely beyond its medieval bounds, visitors still tend to concentrate on the beautiful historic centre, with its magnificent old colleges.

This book, however, shows that Cambridge has so much more to offer. It focuses on walks off the beaten track, covering some of the city's wonderful green spaces, its older and its on-going developments, and the hidden gems that most visitors (and some locals) never see. There are routes through the more rural areas on the city's periphery, and through nearby villages as well as through city communities closer to the centre. Walks also explore the nearby historic towns of Ely and St Ives, both of which are easily accessible from Cambridge.

So, while there is no better way to see the compact city centre than through the fascinating walking tours offered by Cambridge's Blue and Green Badge guides, the walks in this book cover the wider city. We hope that you will enjoy discovering some remarkable aspects of Cambridge and its environs that you may not have known existed.

about the authors

Maggie Hartley, Ruth Meyer, Steve Robertson, Sophie Smiley, Chris Weeds and Cathy Willis are all Cambridge Green Badge tour guides who love welcoming visitors to their wonderful city, and who are delighted to have the opportunity to share some of its hidden secrets.

how to use this book

Each of the 20 walks in this guide is set out in a similar way. They are all introduced with a brief description, including notes on things you will encounter on your walk, and a photograph of a place of interest you might pass along the way.

On the first page of each walk there is a panel of information outlining the distance of the walk, a guide to the walking time, and a brief description of the path conditions

or the terrain you will encounter. A suggested starting point along with the nearest postcode is shown, although postcodes can cover a large area therefore this is just a rough guide.

The major part of each section is taken up with route maps and detailed point-to-point directions for the walk. The route instructions are prefixed by a number in a circle, and the corresponding location is shown on the map.

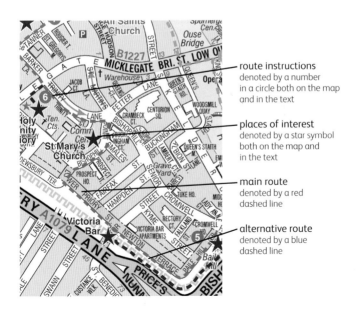

route instructions
denoted by a number in a circle both on the map and in the text

places of interest
denoted by a star symbol both on the map and in the text

main route
denoted by a red dashed line

alternative route
denoted by a blue dashed line

AZ walk one

Early Cambridge

From the market to Castle Mound.

This short walk starts centrally, but quickly takes you away from the modern city to the medieval town, with the chance to see places unknown to visitors, and perhaps even to those who live here. There are several places to pause and look further or to enjoy a break.

Begin in the market where colourful stalls sell their goods every day of the week. In the 18th century, butter was sold here by the yard, for the convenience of college butlers and by the inch, to meet the requirements of students. Milton's Walk beside Christ's Pieces ends up in a narrow passageway known locally as Cut Throat Alley, following the brutal murder here of a local shopkeeper over a hundred years ago. King Street has many pubs and lends its name to a student challenge of drinking a pint of beer in each of them, the so-called King Street Run. Stroll across Jesus Green, one of several large open spaces available for residents and visitors to relax and enjoy – the lungs of Cambridge!

The walk passes the Museum of Cambridge, with a fascinating collection of local artefacts, Kettle's Yard Museum of Modern Art, St Giles' Church and the tiny St Peter's Church. If you have time, any or all are well worth visiting. Return to the centre via narrow alleys and streets that tell the story of early Cambridge.

start / finish	Market Hill
nearest postcode	CB1 0SS
distance	2¼ miles / 3.7 km
time	1 hour
terrain	Pavements and surfaced footpaths. Stepped slope which can be muddy.

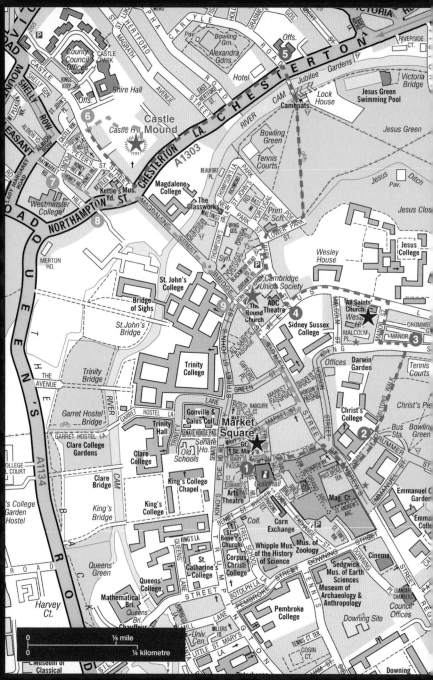

① Facing the market ★ , with your back to the brick-built Guildhall, take the road to the right through Petty Cury, the modern shopping street. Communal cooking was done here before chimneys in smaller houses became common in the 17th century. Turn right at the end, past the front of Christ's College with its brightly decorated gatehouse on the opposite side of the road. Cross over carefully and go down the footpath on the left, between Christ's and the modern shops, emerging beside the bus station.

② Continue on the path straight ahead beside the high wall of Christ's and through a narrow passageway, Milton's Walk. John Milton, 17th century scholar and poet, studied at Christ's for 7 years from the age of 16.

③ At the end, turn left onto King Street. After 200 yards (180 metres) turn right onto Manor Street and left onto Jesus Lane. Almost on the corner as you turn into Jesus Lane is All Saints Church ★ , a tribute to the Victorian Arts and Crafts Movement. When the traffic allows cross over to Jesus College, founded on the site of a 12th-century Benedictine nunnery and where the current Earl of Wessex was an undergraduate.

④ At the third set of traffic lights, turn right onto Park Street, passing a very elegant house set back from the road. The road branches to the right, becoming Lower Park Street, past the Victorian buildings of Park Street School on the left and cottages on the right, which are now student accommodation. At the end is a gap on the left through the railings. Follow the footpath across the wide expanse of Jesus Green leading to the footbridge over the River Cam. Take care on the footpath as it is shared with bicycles. Cross the footbridge and immediately cross the pedestrian crossing.

⑤ Turn left from the crossing and walk to the end of this road, Chesterton Road, with tall houses on the right and views across Jesus Green on the left. Several white 18th-century cottages are on the left. At the traffic lights turn right up Castle Street. Just here, there are several interesting places to visit: St Giles' Church on the corner where Sheriff Picot's wife built a church in Norman times in gratitude for being spared from death, the Museum of Cambridge, Kettle's Yard and the tiny 11th-century St Peter's Church. Look out for the turnpike sign on the wall! Continue up Castle Street.

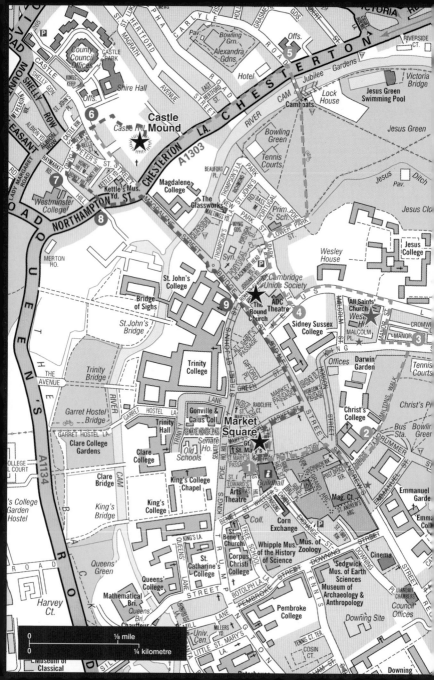

6 Take the footpath to the right just after the Castle Inn. Follow the stepped path to the top of Castle Mound ★ for a wide view of the city and surrounding area. Pause a minute to take in the view. Retrace your steps to Castle Street and cross straight over between the Architect pub and some cottages set back from the road and follow the footpath, Whyman's Lane, to emerge on St Peter's Street. Take a dogleg to the left, crossing over to go down Pound Hill. The former Castle End Mission and Working Men's Club is on the corner – the inspiration of campaigning Christians in Victorian times, who determined to improve the living conditions in this deprived part of town. Note the cobblestones at the edges of Pound Hill, indicating that this is an old road.

7 Before Pound Hill bends to the left down the hill, glance up to the right to see the row of Victorian cottages in Haymarket, but take the footpath to the left between the modern building and the rectangular building on the corner, the former Free School. This path, Honey Hill, is the ironic name for the medieval ditch that was on this site, a dump for rubbish and sewage. Emerge at the end onto Northampton Street. Opposite is a lane to the back of St John's College and on the corner is a former almshouse built under the will of Edmund Storey in 1693. He made provision for poor widows and unsupported women in need, providing assistance and a length of cloth every year in a sad colour.

8 Turn left on Northampton Street, and at the traffic lights cross over to head down Magdalene Street on the right, back into the centre. You might notice a totem pole at the junction which marks the site of the discovery of a hoard of medieval coins. Further down Magdalene Street notice some 600 brass flowers embedded in the pavement. These are the work of the artist Michael Fairfax. Pass the Pickerel Inn on the right, established in 1608, and then cross the river. In earlier times the river was the main drain and numerous barges transported coal, grain and other goods to the many wharves along this part of the river. Beside the bridge was a ducking stool for dunking offenders in the river, not a pleasant experience.

9 As you approach the Round Church ★ continue straight on up Bride Street, becoming Sidney Street, passing Sidney Sussex College behind the high walls on the left. At the junction of Market Street, just before Holy Trinity Church, turn right to lead up to the market and return to the start point.

A-Z walk two

The Medieval Church and the River

The Round Church, the River Cam and
Midsummer Orchard.

This lovely walk starts in the city at the 900-year-old Round Church, leading
through ancient streets and skirting Jesus Green to the River Cam. As you pass
the iron footbridge next to the only lock in Cambridge, look down and you
might be able to see a small sculpture, almost out of view, designed to delight,
inspire and amuse!

The open-air Jesus Green Lido was constructed in the 1920s and is deliberately
long and narrow to give the impression that you are swimming in the open
water of the river itself. Midsummer Common is an ancient grassland nestling
in the heart of Cambridge and you will probably see cattle grazing here. On the
other bank of the river are the boathouses of the town, college and university
rowing crews who are out on the river most days.

The delightful Midsummer Orchard is a small community orchard. Pause
for a picnic here and then stroll back towards the centre of the city, passing
handsome houses that look a little like dolls houses set back from the road.
Jesus College is on the right at the end of a long, walled passage known as
The Chimney, and opposite is All Saints Church, a triumph of Victorian art and
design. Call in if it's open and see dramatic colours on almost every surface.
Pass the ADC Theatre, the oldest university playhouse in the country and return
to the Round Church.

start / finish	Round Church, Bridge Street
nearest postcode	CB2 1UB
distance	2 miles / 3 km
time	1 hour
terrain	Pavements and paved walkways. Short grassy track and shallow steps.

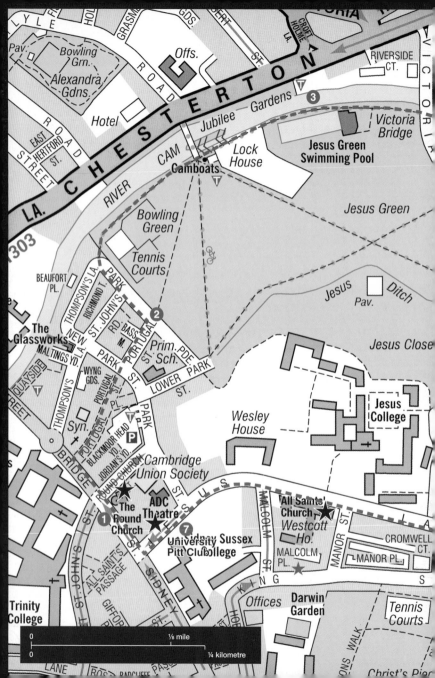

LYLE

Pav.

Bowling
Grn.

Alexandra
Gdns.

HOLE

GRASMERE GDNS.

ALBERT ST

CROFT HOLME LA.

VICTORIA

RIVERSIDE
CT.

Offs.

Hotel

ROAD

EAST
HERTFORD
ST.

ROAD
STREET

LA. CHESTERTON

Jubilee Gardens

③

CAM

Camboats

Lock
House

Victoria
Bridge

RIVER

Jesus Green
Swimming Pool

A303

BEAUFORT
PL.

Bowling
Green

Tennis
Courts

Jesus Green

Jesus

Pav.

Ditch

The
Glassworks

THOMPSON'S LA.

RICHMOND T.

NEW LA.

MALTINGS YD.

ST. JOHN'S

PARK

RD.

ST.

M.

BASS

PORTUGAL

PORTUGAL ST.

Prim.
Sch.

PDE.

LOWER PARK

ST.

②

Jesus Close

Wesley
House

Jesus
College

QUAYSIDE

THOMPSON'S

STREET

WYNG
GDS.

PORTUGAL PL.

Syn.

BLACKMOOR HEAD YD.

JORDAN'S YD.

BRIDGE

PORTUGAL

ST. JOHN'S

ROUND CHURCH ST.

P

PARK

ST.

Cambridge
Union Society

The
Round
Church

ADC
Theatre

①

⑦

University
Pitt Club

Sidney Sussex
College

SIDNEY ST.

ALL SAINT'S
PASSAGE

ST. JOHN'S

Trinity
College

GIFFORD

SIDNEY ST.

KING ST.

MALCOLM ST.

MALCOLM
CT.

MALCOLM
PL.

All Saints'
Church

Westcott
Ho.

MANOR ST.

CROMWELL
CT.

MANOR PL.

A

S

Offices

Darwin
Garden

Tennis
Courts

HOB

SONS WALK

Christ's Pier

LANE

ROS

RADCLIFFE

PAS

0   ⅛ mile

0   ¼ kilometre

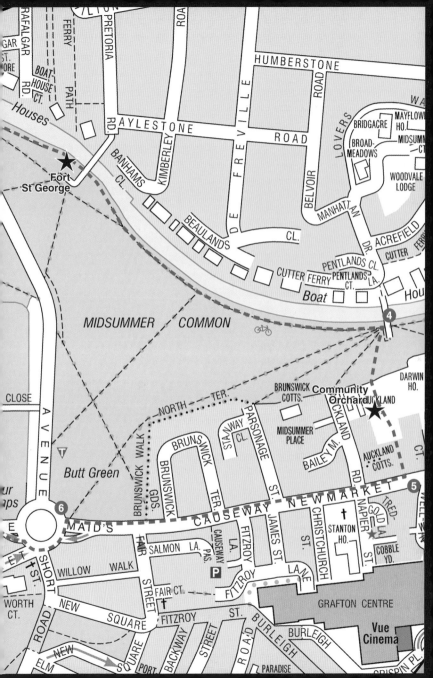

❶ From the Round Church ★ cross over Round Church Street, watching out for other road users. The proper name for this church is the Church of the Holy Sepulchre; built in the 12th century and situated on a Roman road with close proximity to the river, this originally served as a wayfarers' church. Continue along Bridge Street past fine half-timbered buildings, and immediately before St Clement's Church, turn right into Portugal Place, a peaceful well-preserved street, with several different opinions about how it got its name. Cross straight over Park Street and continue to the end.

❷ Turn left onto Park Parade. Jesus Green is on your right, a large green open space enjoyed by residents and visitors alike. At the end of Park Parade cross over and go through the gate onto the footpath beside the River Cam. Continue with the river on your left, past the iron footbridge and the lock. As you pass the corner of the footbridge, look down and you might see a Dinky Door, just out of plain sight.

❸ Go straight on past Jesus Green Lido, the children's playground and under the road bridge. Bicycles use this footpath as well as pedestrians so remember to watch out for them. Continue on the footpath enjoying the views of the river, the houseboats and the boathouses. The common here is called Midsummer Common and is home to the annual Midsummer Fair, one of the longest-established fairs in England. Amongst other events, Midsummer Common hosts bonfire night in November each year and the Strawberry Fair in the early summer. If you feel like a refreshment, the riverside pub immediately beside the path, the Fort St George ★ , dates, in part, from the 16th century. The footbridge next to the pub replaced the ferry that operated across the river here until the 1920s.

❹ Just before the next footbridge across the river, turn to the right and cross the common towards the grassy bank. According to common rights dating from the 12th century, the people of Cambridge are permitted to graze their cattle here so be careful where you walk! Go up the short flight of steps in front of you and through the gate into the peaceful Midsummer Community Orchard ★ . The orchard was set up in 2009 and is tended by volunteers, who plant trees and wild flowers, cut grass and clear weeds. Do remember to close the gate after you. Continue straight ahead through the orchard to the road.

5 Turn right onto Newmarket Road. On the other side of the road is the Buddhist Centre, the former site of Barnwell Theatre. Further along, still on the opposite side of the road, is Christ Church, unusually orientated north to south rather than east to west. The road leads directly into Maid's Causeway, with handsome houses on both sides. It is a highly desirable street today, but in former times it was rundown and the site of several brothels. Midsummer Common appears again behind the railings on the right just before the roundabout – this area is called Butts Green as, in earlier times, men and boys aged over six years old practised their archery here.

6 Go straight ahead at the roundabout onto Jesus Lane. Cross with care as this road can be busy. You might prefer to cross over just before you reach the roundabout using the central island on Maid's Causeway for safety, then turn right and cross Short Street, again using the central island for safety. Continue down Jesus Lane, passing Jesus College on the right and All Saints Church ★ on the left, a treasure trove of Victorian decorative style. If the church is open and you have time, do pop in. Just before the traffic lights, at the junction, notice the elegant house set back from the road. This is Little Trinity, a very fine house dating from 1725.

7 Pass the junction with Park Street with the ADC Theatre on the right. Pass an unusual neoclassical white building, The University Pitt Club ★ , originally designed as a Victorian Roman Baths. It is named after William Pitt, Britain's youngest prime minister who studied at Pembroke College. At the end of Jesus Lane turn right onto Bridge Street, returning to the start point at the Round Church.

AZ walk three

The Kite

From cricket to football on the city centre greens.

This short walk takes you round the kite-shaped area of Cambridge that was developed from fields in the 19th century. There are many things to discover off the beaten tourist track. The walk begins at the University Arms Hotel, grandly facing onto Parker's Piece, where great cricketer Jack Hobbs played.

It then goes down a road with a college on one side, and housing on the other: it moves from University to town. The street names – Adam & Eve Street, Paradise Street and Eden Street – hark back to the market garden, which was situated in this area. The route passes a Unitarian church, designed by Beatrix Potter's cousin and visited by Mahatma Gandhi. You may be able to pop inside. There is then an old Temperance Hall, which was converted into a studio, making puppets for the satirical 1980s television show, *Spitting Image*.

Old shops, pubs and workshops are knitted into the fabric of Victorian terraced housing. Discover the hidden cottages in Orchard Street, some of the prettiest in Cambridge, built in 1830 for the servants of a nearby estate. You might enjoy a drink in a street made famous for its pub crawl, where 18th-century almshouses rub shoulders with popular drinking haunts. The walk ends at a sculpture celebrating the rules of the game of football, established here in Cambridge in 1848.

start	Junction of Regent Street and Park Terrace
nearest postcode	CB2 1AD
finish	*Cambridge Rules* sculpture, Parker's Piece
distance	1¾ miles / 3 km
time	50 minutes
terrain	Pavements and surfaced footpaths.

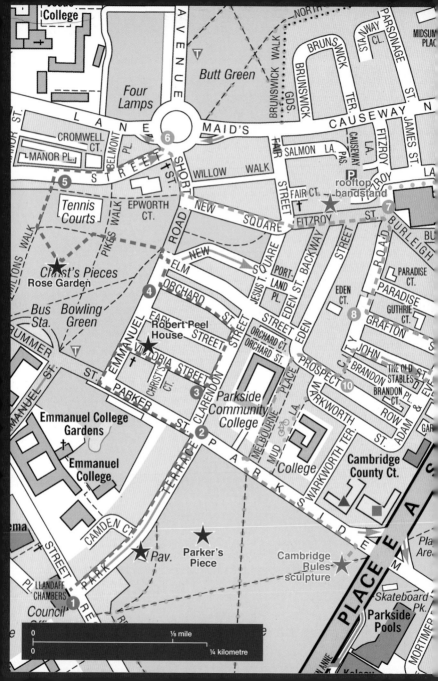

1 Start at the end of Park Terrace, beside the University Arms Hotel, and walk along the side of the building. Past the hotel is Hobbs Pavilion ★, with its blue plaque to one of the country's greatest batsmen, Jack Hobbs, who was born in poverty very near this spot. The large, green expanse on the right is Parker's Piece ★, named after a Trinity College cook who leased the land in the 16th century. Continue along Park Terrace, with its handsome row of 19th-century houses with fine balconies.

2 Turn left at Parker Street. Walk alongside a large red-brick building known as 'the Hostel', part of Emmanuel College. Turn right onto Emmanuel Road. Pass the Unitarian church, visited by Mahatma Gandhi in 1931. Take the first right into Victoria Street. On the left, you will see the bijou Robert Peel House ★ which used to be a police jail. Towards the end of the street, on your left, is a tall red-brick building, the Victoria Hall (1884), originally built as a Temperance Hall. More recently, it was a workshop for the TV comedy *Spitting Image*.

3 Turn left onto Clarendon Street. Two streets down on the left is Orchard Street, one of the most charming streets in Cambridge. On one side are cottages built for the servants of a big estate house, now demolished. They had no upstairs windows at the back, so as not to overlook their master's land. The beautiful mansard roofs curve gently, and the tiny gardens are filled with hollyhocks and wisteria in the summer.

4 At the bottom of Orchard Street is Emmanuel Road, turn right and then use the crossing to go over to Christ's Pieces. Keep straight ahead, and take a path on the left to visit a rose garden ★ dedicated to Diana, Princess of Wales. Take a path on the right, which heads towards a high wall, the boundary with Christ's College, where the poet John Milton studied. Keep going right, beside a play area and tennis courts, then through a narrow alley, Milton's Walk.

5 At King Street, cross the road and look back at the pub sign above the door of the Champion of the Thames, honouring those who 'make drinking a pleasure', and urging them to 'enjoy it and still remain gentlemen'. Its unaltered 19th-century interior is one of the finest in East Anglia. As you face Milton's Walk, from where you have just come, head left on King Street. Further on there are two sets of almshouses, one built in 1790.

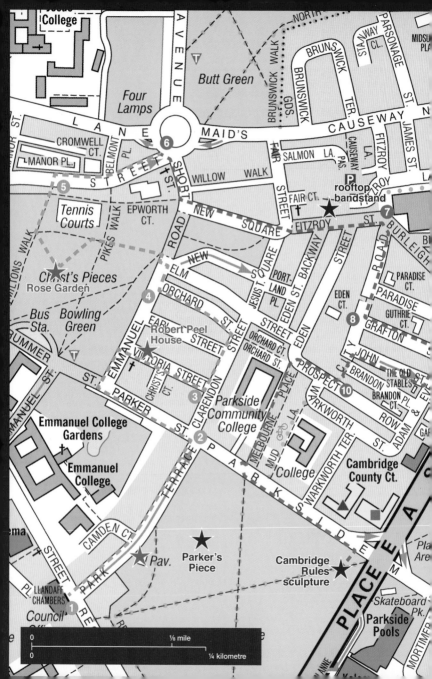

College

Four
Lamps

Butt Green

NORTH

BRUNSWICK WALK

BRUNSWICK GDS.

BRUNSWICK

BRUNSWICK TER.

STANWAY CL.

PARSONAGE

MIDSU
PL

ST.

LANE

MAID'S

CAUSEWAY

ST. JAMES ST.

CROMWELL CT.

MANOR PL.

MANOR ST.

BELMONT PL.

STREET

SHORT ST.

WILLOW WALK

FAIR STREET

SALMON LA.

CAUSEWAY PAS.

FAIR CT.

FITZROY LA.

FITZROY ST.

5

Tennis
Courts

PIKES WALK

EPWORTH CT.

NEW

SQUARE

FITZROY

P rooftop
bandstand

★

ST.

7

BURLEIGH

B

LIONS WALK

Christ's Pieces
Rose Garden

★

ROAD

NEW

ELM

ORCHARD

SOUTH

JESUS T. SQUARE

PORT-
LAND
PL.

EDEN ST. BACKWAY

STREET

EDEN CT.

PARADISE CT.

PARADISE

GUTHRIE
CT.

ROAD

8

Bus
Sta.

Bowling
Green

4

STREET

EARL

VICTORIA STREET

Robert Peel
House

STREET

ORCHARD ST.

ORCHARD CT.

EDEN

STREET

GRAFTON

CITY

JOHN

ST.

THE OLD
STABLES

DRUMMER ST.

EMMANUEL ST.

EMMANUEL STREET

CHRIST'S CT.

3

Parkside
Community
College

PLACE

PROSPECT

BRANDON

10

BRANDON PL.

ROW

&

Emmanuel College
Gardens

PARKER ST.

CLARENDON ST.

2

MELBOURNE PLACE

MUD LA.

WARKWORTH

STREET

WARKWORTH TER.

ADAM

GAF

Cambridge
County Ct.

Emmanuel
College

TERRACE

PARK

CAMDEN CT.

ROAD

PARKSIDE

College

▲

■

ema

STREET

PARK

★ Pav.

★
Parker's
Piece

★
Cambridge
Rules
sculpture

PLACE

E

Pla
Are

LLANDAFF
CHAMBERS

PL.

Council
Off

1

ROAD

Skateboard
Pk.

Parkside
Pools

ANNE

MORTIMER

0   ⅛ mile

0   ¼ kilometre

6 At the roundabout, turn right onto Short Street, then use the zebra crossing at the end of the street to walk over to New Square. The attractive houses round three sides of the square are owned by Jesus College. Continue walking ahead, going along Fitzroy Street, a busy pedestrianized shopping area. On the left is a fine building, originally a department store. Notice the bandstand on the roof ★ , where concerts used to be held to entertain the shoppers.

7 Turn right at City Road. At No. 36A look for the small signs of F. R. Leach, Glazier and Painter and N. E. Leach, Milliner. The house originally had workshops at the back. It belonged to an important local Arts and Crafts company, which worked with people like William Morris. Their skills can be seen in places such as the nearby Jesus College Chapel, and All Saints Church. It typifies the way people lived above their shops and workplaces in Victorian days.

8 At Grafton Street turn left. Numbers 4–7, built in the mid-19th century, look like almshouses, with mysterious crests on them; they may have been built with stone from the castle which was being demolished at the time. Go past the Jubilee Chapel on your left and turn right at Adam & Eve Street. Walk alongside the old tram depot, now a pub. This was the terminus for the horse-drawn trams which transported locals until 1914.

9 Turn right down John Street, back to City Road, and then left through a pedestrian path to the Free Press pub. Inside, you will discover part of a rowing boat which crashed before it even got to the start of the race. It carries the words of the boat's cox, whose steering caused the collision, saying 'All my own work'.

10 Go right along Prospect Row. Then left down the lovely Melbourne Place, where houses face onto a hidden, traffic-free path. On reaching Parkside, go right to the crossing, and then left along the edge of Parker's Piece. Just before the crossroads, turn right onto the green. Your walk ends at the memorial ★ to The Laws of the University Football Club to the left of the path. In 1848, a group of students nailed a set of rules of football to a tree nearby. The modern game started here!

A-Z walk four

In Darwin's Footsteps

Botanic Garden, Coe Fen and University Colleges.

This circular walk starts across riverside commons, where local farmers still exercise ancient rights to graze cattle. It combines the hidden remains of the old market town with some of the University's most iconic – and controversial – faculty buildings. You will pass an old water mill, an oast house and a granary. Pause to look at the gates to Newnham College, the second university college founded for women and the basis of Virginia Woolf's essay *A Room of her Own*.

Stroll through the Arts Faculty site, with its array of modern architecture, including the History Faculty, Stirling's ziggurat, and Norman Foster's Faculty of Law building. Walk in the footsteps of the laundresses who scrubbed the dons' sheets, and perhaps picnic on their green, where Charles Darwin studied beetles. You will return along one of the prettiest lanes in Cambridge, to Trumpington Street where you will see strange runnels; their mystery will be revealed when you reach the stunning Hobson's Conduit memorial.

You may want to call in at the Fitzwilliam Museum, one of nine free museums owned by the University, and a treasure trove of painting, classical artefacts, pottery and much more. Returning alongside the conduit, with its handsome villas and detached gardens, your walk finishes at the beautiful Botanic Garden, where you could visit their tea rooms.

start / finish	Cambridge University Botanic Garden, Brookside
nearest postcode	CB2 1JE
distance	2½ miles / 4 km
time	1 hour
terrain	Pavements and paths, sometimes with puddles. Steps.

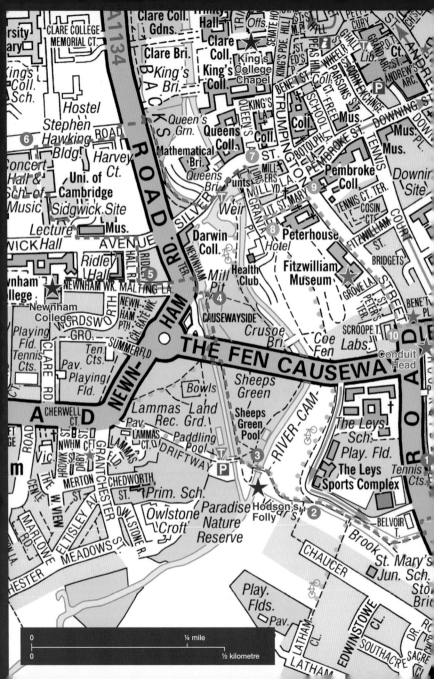

1 From the entrance to the Botanic Garden ★ on Bateman Street, turn left onto Trumpington Road. Use the crossing to cross Trumpington Road then continue along the road. At the cattle grid and gate, turn right and walk alongside a brick wall on Coe Fen. Bear right when the path reaches a small stream, and walk around the back of The Leys school (the home of the original Mr Chips, from the 1939 film).

2 Keep left when the path forks and cross a small bridge. You may see egrets, herons and occasionally kingfishers here. Ahead of you is a river bridge. As you walk over the bridge, look left to see the remains of Hodson's Folly ★ , a little secret garden, with its tiny ruined temple and hidden boat house. This was created by a college butler, born in poverty in Liverpool, who made a fortune; it was his garden of Eden, where his daughter used to swim.

3 Go straight ahead till you reach a low bridge over a tributary. (There are toilets, café and a paddling pool on the far side should you want a detour.) Turn right before this bridge and walk to the road with the stream on your left. At Fen Causeway, use the crossing to cross the road, and continue to follow the stream on your left.

4 At a water mill (now a restaurant) turn left and walk in front of the mill, where diners sit. In front of you is a converted oast house. Use the crossing to reach it, then turn right and immediately left along Malting Lane, almost unchanged for a couple of hundred years. At the end of Malting Lane, you can make a detour to the end of Newnham Walk to see the beautiful gates of Newnham College ★ ; poet Sylvia Plath did postgraduate studies here.

5 Back on Malting Lane, turn along Ridley Hall Road and walk alongside this Gothic theological college. At the leafy Sidgwick Avenue, turn left. Walk between 19th-century college buildings on the left, and the modern Arts Faculty on your right. Turn right into this new campus. Walk past the Lady Mitchell Hall, up some steps and under a building raised on columns. There are some remarkable modern buildings by famous 20th-century architects.

6 At West Road, turn right and walk to Queen's Road. Use the pedestrian crossing to reach the gates to King's College. There is a fine view of the chapel ★ on the left. Pick up the path winding diagonally right across 'The Backs' to Queen's College. In spring, this area is carpeted in flowers. At Silver Street, take the crossing then turn left. Stop on the bridge to enjoy a view of the Mathematical Bridge and also the Mill Pond.

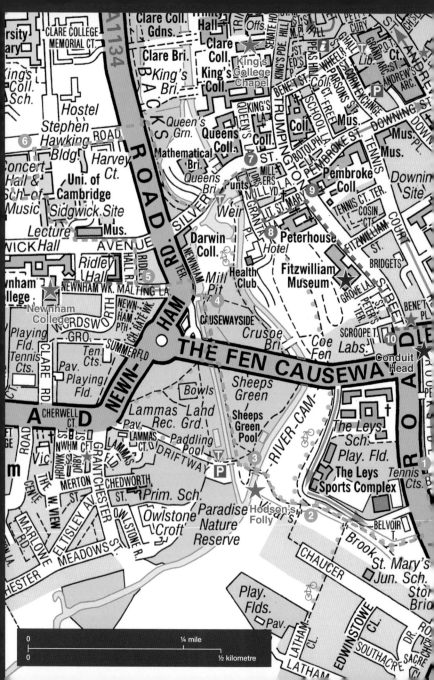

7 Take a right beyond the Anchor pub and go down Laundress Lane. Half a bike juts out of a high wall, workshops and rubbish bins jostle. At the end, look up: a notice from 1857 announces that carriages are forbidden. You may want to turn right and stop for a drink at the Mill Pond, or a picnic on Laundress Green where Darwin used to hunt beetles. The college opposite is named after him. Continue on Granta Place, past the brutalist Graduate Centre.

8 Turn left up Little St Mary's Lane, with its charming cottages. Look up to see the sign of a half moon, a reminder of an old pub. The Little St Mary's Church graveyard, nestled up against Peterhouse College, is a wildlife haven and a lovely place to sit awhile. Pop into the church and look for a plaque which reveals the secret of where the American flag originated.

9 Turn right at Trumpington Street, looking across at Pembroke College. It may be open for visitors. Runnels run beside the road, the legacy of a remarkable feat of engineering which brought clean water to the people of Cambridge. Pass the Fitzwilliam Museum ★. You may want to explore its amazing collections. Notice the splendid golden pineapples in the railings. Opposite, is the impressive Judge Institute, a colourful refurbishment of the old Addenbrooke's Hospital, founded for the poor of Cambridge.

10 At the junction with Lensfield Road, cross carefully to the magnificent 17th-century fountain, a hexagonal monument to Thomas Hobson ★. He was a local entrepreneur who helped build a conduit to bring clean water to the town. It is crowned by a golden pinecone – not another pineapple! From here you can look across to the gothic buildings of The Leys school. Turn right, after the fountain, onto Brookside. The last leg of the walk takes you alongside the old canal, between elegant villas and their waterside gardens. Notice the blue plaques at No. 18 to a remarkable couple – a suffragist, and her husband, an MP and Postmaster-General who introduced parcel post and telegrams, and happened to be blind. Your walk ends back where you started, with a final plaque to John Stevens Henslow, the scholar who turned down a voyage on the *Beagle* to establish these gardens.

A̶Z walk five

Mill Road

The Victorian street with a modern vibe.

This walk explores a fascinating area beyond the medieval world of the University, to where rapid expansion occurred from the mid-19th century after the opening of the railway. It takes you through some rich social history in a place where dense housing, workplaces, crime and aspiration sat cheek by jowl.

In the grounds of Parkside Pool, the walk passes a sculpture of three naked bathers, modestly surrounded by a circle of greenery. Further on, in a beautiful Victorian cemetery, there are seven hidden sculptures, inscribed with poems about birds; these nestle amongst the trees and ivy-clad graves in a natural oasis. If you are in need of refreshment, there is a little gap in the wall which goes through to the garden of The Cambridge Blue pub.

The walk passes the old workhouse, which served as a hospital for troops evacuated from Dunkirk during the Second World War; more recently it was a maternity hospital, and now a retirement home. There is an old sausage factory, a brewery and a bath house. Mill Road was said to cater for every need, from birth to death!

Highlights of the second part of the walk include the David Parr House, beautifully decorated by a 19th-century craftsman (booking required). The walk ends near a magnificent new eco mosque, partly inspired by King's College Chapel, where you could sit awhile in its lovely garden.

start	At the centre of Parker's Piece
nearest postcode	CB1 1NA
finish	Cambridge Central Mosque, Mill Road
distance	2¼ miles / 3.6 km
time	1 hour
terrain	Pavements and paved walkways.

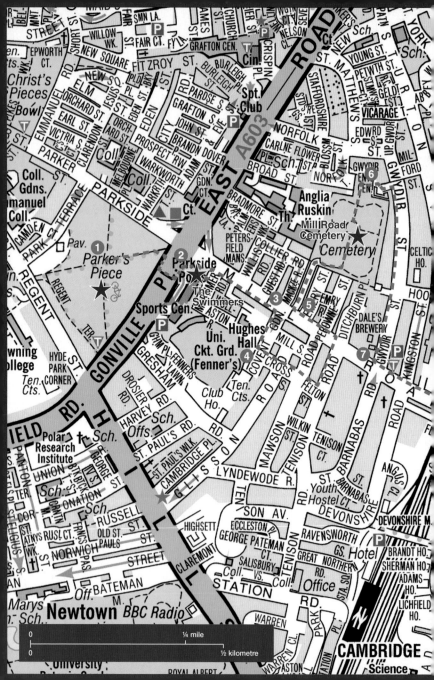

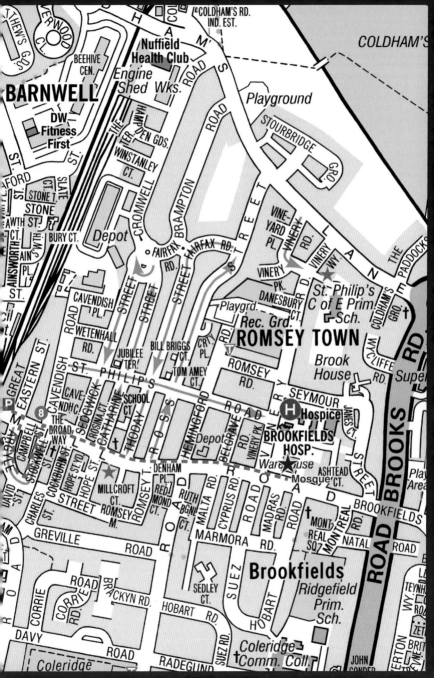

1 Start at the centre of Parker's Piece ★, the large green at the western end of Mill Road. A lamppost carries the graffiti 'Reality Checkpoint'. This is the end of the student bubble and the beginning of the town. Stand with your back to Park Terrace and take the path diagonally left towards the corner of the park. You will pass a sculpture commemorating the establishment of the Rules of Football here in 1848. At Gonville Place, cross over to the green in front of the swimming pool.

2 Walk diagonally across Donkey Common to the left of Parkside Pool. There is a sculpture of bathers – *The Swimmers* ★ – hidden amongst the trees and bushes on your right. At Mortimer Road, turn left, and then right onto Mill Road. This is a vibrant, cosmopolitan area, full of independent shops and eateries. It developed in the 19th century when the railway arrived.

3 Turn right into Covent Garden, where an old sausage factory has been converted into flats. Look carefully at the wall alongside the supermarket and notice the small crater-shaped holes in the bricks. These were made by children scraping their pennies while queuing for the cinema, which preceded the shop. The residents have put blue plaques in their windows commemorating the Victorian people who lived here.

4 Turn left at Cross Street, then cross over Mawson Road onto Felton Street. Notice the old stables and workshops, and the faded advertisement painted on the wall. Turn left onto Tenison Road. On the right is Bolton's Warehouse, with its high hoist for pulling goods off horse-drawn carts. At Mill Road, cross over to see Ditchburn Place, the old workhouse. With Ditchburn Place behind you, turn right, back along Mill Road.

5 Turn right into a tree-lined avenue (just before Mackenzie Road, through black wrought-iron gates), which leads to Mill Road Cemetery ★ . At the end of the avenue is a flint-built cottage. There are seven sculptures hidden within the cemetery, inscribed with poems about birds. Take the path on the right, and then the main path on the left which leads to a central circle. Continue ahead, and just before the exit turn right and leave through a gate in the wall.

6 Go through the Gwydir Street Enterprise Centre, a collection of old workshops. At Gwydir Street turn right. Stop at No. 186 where a Victorian craftsman used to live. He decorated his house with wall paintings, tiles and prints in the style of William Morris. This treasure was recently discovered and conserved. It is next to a 1920s bath house, and opposite Dales, a splendid, converted brewery.

7 At Mill Road, turn left. Notice the fine Victorian 'Free Library' building, a red-brick temple. Go over the railway bridge and turn right at Argyle Street, a terraced crescent. Turn left at Stockwell Street and return to Mill Road. Cross the road to see a sculpture on the corner of Cavendish Road in the shape of a giant 'R' for Romsey and Railway.

8 From Cavendish Road, turn right along Mill Road, with the Baptist Church on your right across the road. After a third of a mile (600 metres), on your left you will find the magnificent Cambridge Central Mosque ★ , with its arching wooden pillars. It may be open for visitors, and it's generally possible to sit and enjoy the exquisite little garden at the front. Retrace your steps along Mill Road, crossing it at the pedestrian crossing, to catch the bus from outside The Royal Standard pub back to the city centre.

AZ walk six

Three Burial Grounds

Resting places through the ages.

This is a circular walk starting from the top of Castle Hill, where the Romans, and later the Normans, established a settlement that began the city of Cambridge. All that remains today is the 33-foot (10-metre) high mound, Castle Mound, which for Cambridge is an unusually high spot with wide views over the city and beyond from the top.

Histon Road Cemetery was established in 1843 and was one of the first to be open to those of any or no religion. As the nonconformist burial place for the town, all levels of society are represented from all parts of the town, together with many babies and young children, reminding us of the high infant mortality rate in Victorian times. The Ascension Parish Burial Ground, dubbed the brainiest cemetery in Britain, is the final resting place for some of Cambridge University's most influential astronomers, engineers, poets and philosophers, including several Nobel Prize-winners and Knights of the Realm. This former chapel of rest is now the workshop of a letter carver.

The walk continues round the University Observatory, established in 1823 and now part of the site of the Institute of Astronomy, continuing past the Isaac Newton Centre for Mathematical Sciences, an international research institute for mathematics and its many applications. Return to the start crossing the site of a large Anglo-Saxon cemetery in use from the 5th to the 7th century.

start / finish	Castle Hill, Castle Street
nearest postcode	CB3 0AJ
distance	3½ miles / 5.5 km
time	1 hour 30 minutes
terrain	Pavements and surface footpaths. Some dirt and grassy paths and steps. Shared cycle paths.

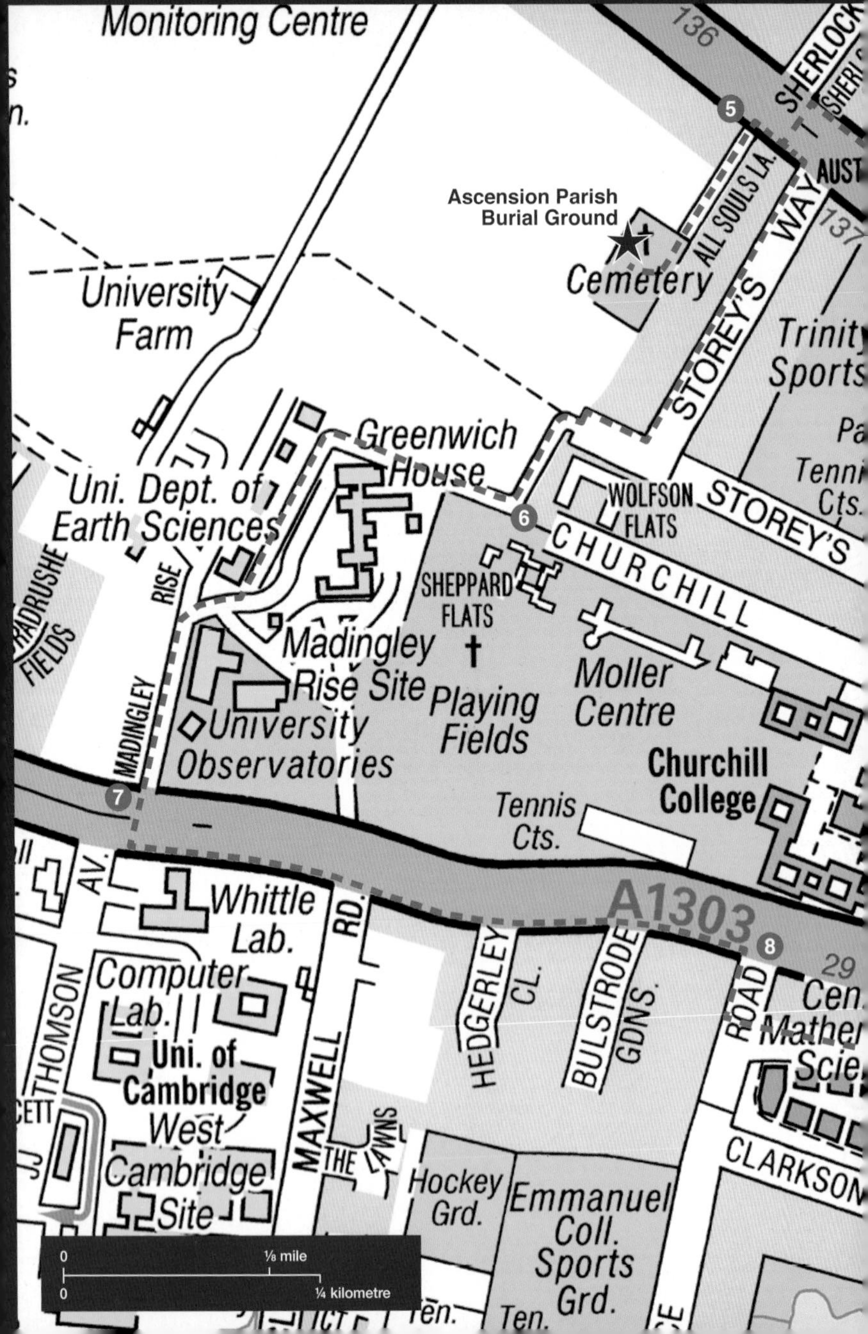

Monitoring Centre

136

SHERLOCK

SHERI

5

AUST

Ascension Parish
Burial Ground

ALL SOULS LA.

137

Cemetery

University
Farm

STOREY'S WAY

Trinity
Sports

Pa

Tenni
Cts.

Greenwich
House

Uni. Dept. of
Earth Sciences

WOLFSON
FLATS

6

CHURCHILL

STOREY'S

RISE

MADRUSHE

FIELDS

SHEPPARD
FLATS

Madingley
Rise Site

Playing
Fields

Moller
Centre

MADINGLEY

University
Observatories

Churchill
College

7

Tennis
Cts.

A1303

8

29

AV.

Whittle
Lab.

THOMSON

Computer
Lab.

Uni. of
Cambridge

West

Cambridge
Site

MAXWELL RD.

THE LAWNS

HEDGERLEY CL.

BULSTRODE GDNS.

ROAD

Cen.
Mathe
Scie

Hockey
Grd.

Emmanuel
Coll.
Sports
Grd.

CLARKSON

CETT

Ten.

Ten.

| 0 | ⅛ mile |
| 0 | ¼ kilometre |

Barn Comm.
Cen.
GOODWIN CT.
CHESTERTON MILLS
RICHARD NEWCOMBE CT.
St. Lukes C of E Prim. Sch.
WORTH RD.
GEORGES RD.
Works HO.
RACKHAM RD.
4
SYDENHAM T.
Rec. Grd.
LINDEN CL.
SUPANEO CT.
OXFORD CL.
RICHMOND RD.
HALIFAX
CANTERBURY
CANTER BURY CL.
DANIELS HO.
GIBBONS HO. CHELSEA M.
FRENCH'S
102
ST. CBY CT.
ST. CHRIST.
ST. STPN.
PL.
WESTF.RD
NORTH ST.
ROAD
139
BERMUDA RD.
BERMUDA
Histon Road Cemetery
3
WESTFIELD LA.
CHAMBERLIN CT.
ST.
Hall rd.
R
O
A
D
PRIORY RD.
BENSON ST.
CRANWELL
BEN-SON CT.
CT. PL.
PRCE WM CT.
Halls of Res.
Fitzwilliam Coll.
Coll.
VICTORIA
HILDA
SEARLE
ST LUKE
WAY
Murray Edwards College
BUCKINGHAM RD.
MT. PLEASANT
P
Coun. Offs.
CASTLE PK.
2
CLARE ST.
ATH HALL
HER
OADWAY WAY
St. Edmund's College †
SHELLY ROW
CASTLE
JN.SP. Offs.
Shire Hall
1
MAGRAT
STOREY'S CRESCENT
FULLER WY.
LARMOR
THE CRES.
BENIANS CT. DR.
Lucy Cavendish College
MARGARET RD.
LADY
MT.P.LINK
ALBION ROW
SHY. GN.
ST. JN.
ST. PETER'S
ST.PETR'S
ST. ST.
WTMN'S
CWTMN'S
VLA ST.
Castle Hill †
LADY MARGARET RD.
MKT.
RD.
Coll.
HAY. HL.
MRD.
HONEY HL.
KETLS
YD.
11
NORTHAMPTON STREET
13
R
O
A
D
Q
U
E
WOLFSON COURT
Sch.
Pav.
burial ground
10
9
ROAD
St. John's Coll. Playing Flds.
St. John's College
ARKSON CL.
CROFT PL.

1 Starting in the car park at the top of Castle Hill ★, you might like to climb the stepped slope to the top of Castle Mound and enjoy the view of the city, the University and the colleges. On a clear day Ely Cathedral is visible to the north. Retrace your steps and take the road between the old, brick-built, registry office and Shire Hall, turning to the right at the end and following the footpath towards a short flight of steps. At the bottom of the steps cross the small car park.

2 Continue straight ahead on St Luke's Street. The tall spire of St Luke's Church is straight ahead. Take the next turn on the left into Searle Street and, at the end, cross over Victoria Road. This can be a busy road so take care here. Straight in front of you is the gate into Histon Road Cemetery ★. Follow the dirt path round to the other gate at the opposite end when you are ready to leave the cemetery. The graves here are largely those of local tradespeople, some of whom have very impressive monuments. As you leave, notice the Grade II listed neo-Gothic lodge at the gate, now a private residence.

3 Turn right and walk along Histon Road to a pedestrian crossing. Cross over and turn back to a narrow gateway on the right that takes you into a recreation ground. The path is decorated with colourful metal birds flying overhead. Where the path widens out into the grassy area, take the right-hand path and continue straight ahead, emerging onto Richmond Road via

another path and gateway decorated with metallic birds.

4 Turn left, and at the end of Richmond Road turn right onto Huntingdon Road. Just after the junction with Marion Close, cross over Huntingdon Road at the pedestrian crossing and enter the path to the right leading to the Ascension Parish Burial Ground ★. Designated a city wildlife site, the graveyard is delightfully overgrown and a place of peace. Take your time reading the inscriptions. When you are ready, retrace your steps to Huntingdon Road.

5 Turn right, then right again into Storey's Way, a broad road lined with established family houses. Where the road divides, take the bend round to the right. After about 100 yards (90 metres) the road becomes a footpath and cycle way. Continue straight on and turn left again just before the wooden fencing across the path. This is now University land so be sure to stay on the footpath.

6 The path turns to the right and then divides. Follow the tarmac path signposted 'cycle way' to the Cavendish Laboratory. This path curves round the Institute of Astronomy, a department of the University engaged in teaching and research in the fields of theoretical and observational astronomy. Where the cycle path meets a road, turn right on the footpath alongside a paddock to Madingley Road at the end.

7 Cross Madingley Road at the pedestrian crossing and turn left to follow Madingley Road back towards the city centre. On the right is the West Cambridge Site of the University. Several University departments have relocated here in recent years and the roads are named after Cambridge scientists: JJ Thomson Avenue after Sir Joseph J Thomson, British physicist and Nobel Laureate in Physics, credited with the discovery of the electron. As you go down Madingley Road, cross over Clerk Maxwell Road, named after James Clerk Maxwell, Scottish mathematician and scientist responsible for the theory of electromagnetism.

8 Turn right into Wilberforce Road. A short distance down the road on the left is a footpath leading you alongside the University Centre for Mathematical Sciences. Since Sir Isaac Newton was Lucasian Professor (1669–1696), mathematics teaching and research here have been enhanced by a string of brilliant mathematicians. Most current Faculty members are leading international authorities on their subject. Follow the footpath as it turns right, emerging on Clarkson Road.

9 Turn left. At the end of Clarkson Road, cross over Grange Road using the pedestrian crossing, and you will see an iron gate in the hedge. Go through the gate into the playing fields of St John's College. (Note that dogs are not permitted here. If you have a

dog, turn left along Grange Road. At the T-junction, turn right onto Madingley Road and, at the end, turn left to rejoin the route at step 10.) You are now entering a burial ground ★ dating from the Anglo-Saxon period, a mixed inhumation and cremation cemetery of which nothing is visible now. This land is private but pedestrians are usually welcome to cross the land, keeping to the footpath. At the end of the path on the far side of the playing field, emerge through the iron gate and turn left, heading to the small roundabout at the end of this road, Queen's Road.

10 You might be able to glance through the metal gates on the opposite side of the main road into the grounds of St John's College. After the roundabout, continue along Northampton Street past the red-brick building of Westminster College, a theological college of the United Reformed Church. Cross Pound Hill. The pub on the corner, The Punter, is a former coaching inn.

11 Turn left up Pound Hill, crossing it at the bend to stay on the pavement. At the corner is Honey Hill Mews, euphemistically so called as in earlier times the town's nightsoil was dumped here. Continue up Pound Hill, cross the road and go up Whyman's Lane opposite, emerging on Castle Hill opposite the pub, The Castle Inn. Cross here to return to the start point.

A̶Z̶ walk seven

Hobson's Conduit

A walk along the brook from the city to its source.

Hobson's Conduit was created by a group of town and university philanthropists in the early 17th century to bring fresh water into Cambridge from the springs at Nine Wells. A drinking fountain erected in the market square was later replaced and the original was moved to the bottom of Lensfield Road. It is known as the Conduit Head, and the walk starts here.

The path beside the brook goes along the aptly named Brookside, between elegant villas and their private waterside gardens. The brook then runs by the western edge of the Botanic Garden before forking left, and the path beside the brook becomes a rural idyll. It is impossible to believe that you are in the midst of a built-up area, walking parallel to the main road from the centre of Cambridge to the suburb of Trumpington.

You eventually reach Long Road then turn into the Biomedical Campus, which combines Addenbrooke's Hospital with state-of-the-art research facilities. The walk through the campus passes beautiful modern buildings and uplifting green areas before exiting into fields. A short walk takes you to the small Nine Wells nature reserve where Hobson's Conduit rises from the chalk. Returning across the fields, you walk through a modern housing estate to reach the main road and finally the bus station at the front of Addenbrooke's Hospital, where you can catch a bus back to the city centre.

start	Conduit Head, at the junction of Lensfield Road and Trumpington Road
nearest postcode	CB2 1EN
finish	Addenbrooke's Hospital bus station
distance	4¾ miles / 7.5 km
time	2 hours
terrain	Pavements and paths. Dirt paths which can be muddy. Some steps.

This Structure stood upon the
Market Hill and served as a
Conduit from 1614–1856 in which
year it was Re-erected on this
spot by Public Subscription

HOBSON'S CONDUIT

IN 1614, A JOINT ENTERPRISE OF THE
UNIVERSITY AND THE TOWN OF CAMBRIDGE
BROUGHT A SUPPLY OF RUNNING WATER INTO
THE TOWN FROM SPRINGS AT GREAT SHELFORD.
THOMAS HOBSON, THE CARRIER (1544–1631)
WAS A BENEFACTOR OF THE SCHEME AND FOR
THAT REASON THE WATERCOURSE BECAME KNOWN
AS HOBSON'S CONDUIT.

THIS MONUMENT MARKS THE END OF THE
ARTIFICIAL WATERCOURSE. FROM THIS POINT
THE WATER RUNS IN CULVERTS TO RE-APPEAR
IN RUNNELS IN TRUMPINGTON STREET AND ST.
ANDREW'S STREET. OTHER CULVERTS FEED
PONDS IN CERTAIN OF THE COLLEGES.

FROM 1614 TO 1856 THE MONUMENT
STOOD UPON MARKET HILL WHERE IT
SERVED AS A FOUNTAIN. IN THE LATTER
YEAR, FOLLOWING THE PROVISION OF
A PIPED SUPPLY OF WATER BY THE
CAMBRIDGE WATER COMPANY, THE
FOUNTAIN WAS MOVED TO THIS SITE.
IT WAS RECONDITIONED IN 1967.

THIS PLAQUE WAS ERECTED BY THE
HOBSON'S CONDUIT TRUSTEES AND
UNVEILED BY THE MAYOR OF CAMBRIDGE
COUNCILLOR W. N. BRADFORD J.P.
ON
25 APRIL 1967.

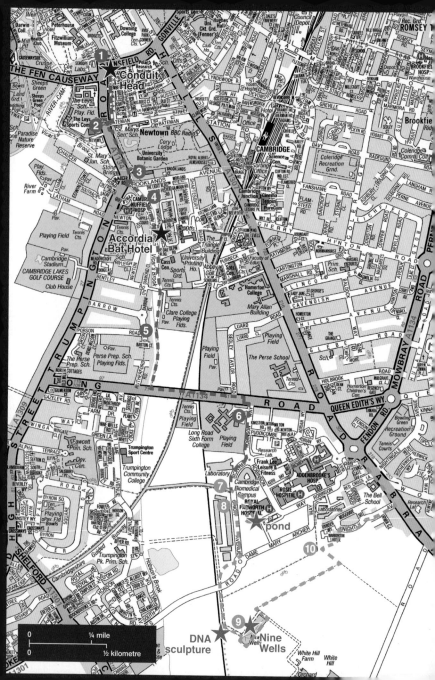

1 Start at Hobson's Conduit on Lensfield Road. After admiring the magnificent Conduit Head ★, walk a few paces up Lensfield Road to turn right into Brookside. The blue plaques at No. 18 are tributes to a suffragist, and to her blind husband, an MP and Postmaster-General who introduced parcel post. At the end of Brookside, cross the small road and turn right towards the entrance to the wonderful Cambridge University Botanic Garden.

2 Ignoring the entrance until another occasion, turn left onto the main road alongside the brook, which forms the western edge of the Botanic Garden. Passing old entrances to the Garden, you can see the lovely ironwork bridges and gates. Shortly before the next junction, the path beside the brook forks left; go between narrow bollards to follow it. At the end of the path are a few steps taking you up to Brooklands Avenue.

3 It is possible to cross Brooklands Avenue at that point, then pass through more narrow bollards and down a few steps to the brook side. However, it would be safer to turn right, walk to the junction and cross at the traffic lights. Turn back down Brooklands Avenue and turn right into the car park, and up to the entry gate to the path alongside the brook.

4 The beautiful path winds beneath trees and next to flowers and reeds on the brook side, with allotments to the right, for roughly half a mile (1 km); it is difficult to believe that you are still in the city. You may see the Accordia Bat Hotel ★ on the other side of a small bridge across the brook, and encounter other walkers and joggers along the route. In wet weather it can be muddy; take care not to slip.

5 At the end of the wooded path turn left and cross the bridge over the brook. Turn right to walk along the edge of the field until you reach Long Road, onto which you turn left. Walk down the road until you can cross at the pedestrian lights. A few paces further on, turn right onto Robinson Way, where the signs announce that you are entering Addenbrooke's Hospital (founded elsewhere in Cambridge in 1766 through the bequest of a university alumnus).

6 Continue along Robinson Way until you reach a roundabout; take the third exit, Francis Crick Avenue (named after one of the discoverers of the DNA double helix), signposted to the Research Quarter. You will pass interesting modern buildings housing the MRC Laboratory of Molecular Biology to your right and Astra Zeneca headquarters to your left. Cross the road, going left at the traffic lights to take a short detour, heading directly towards Royal Papworth Hospital – the leading heart hospital in the country.

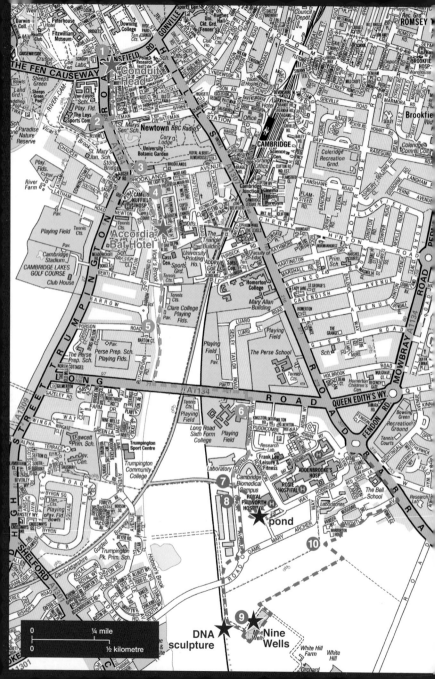

7 The path takes you around the front of Papworth to a lovely pond ★, complete with ducks and reeds, where you can sit and rest. It might be possible to get some refreshments from the Papworth cafeteria, or from nearby food and coffee vans. Return to the front of Papworth and turn left to skirt round another green area.

8 Rejoin Francis Crick Avenue and turn left towards the next roundabout. At the roundabout, take the cycle and pedestrian path to the right, which passes under the road bridge. Carry on straight up the path to see the metal DNA double helix sculpture ★ which marks the one thousandth mile of cycleway, before retracing a few steps and turning right onto the path to Nine Wells.

9 Entering the Nine Wells Local Nature Reserve ★, you will find many possible (and potentially muddy) paths to explore; try to find Hobson's Monument near the southern corner of the reserve. After exploring the reserve, exit from the northern corner. Go straight ahead for a short distance before taking the right turn and following the tree-lined path to its end (½ mile / 640 metres). Turn left and after 170 yards (160 metres), cross a small bridge into a housing estate.

10 Follow the paved path until you turn right onto Knightly Avenue, which takes you to the main Babraham Road. Turn left and carry on to the roundabout where you will see the older main entrance of the hospital campus (dating from the 1960s) on your left. Shortly before the roundabout, turn left into the bus station, where you will find frequent buses to take you back to the centre of town.

A₂ walk eight

'Yet Stands the Church Clock'

The River Cam and Grantchester.

This bucolic walk through hidden local nature reserves and along green riverbanks will convince you that you are in the deepest countryside, rather than on the outskirts of the city.

The walk starts a short distance from the city centre and follows a brook across Coe Fen and Sheep's Green – two of the many greens of the city, inhabited from spring to autumn by grazing cattle. You cross small bridges over the river before walking through the Paradise Local Nature Reserve on the riverbanks. A further short walk through city streets leads to Grantchester Meadows. The route takes you along the river edge of the meadows before finally leading you to the village of Grantchester, beloved by poets Lord Byron and Rupert Brooke.

You could choose to explore the village (and its pubs) before following the walk to the old church, the Orchard and its famous tearoom, the Mill Pond and, finally, the quiet green haven of the Byron's Pool Local Nature Reserve where the eponymous poet reputedly swam. From there, the path takes you across Trumpington Meadows to a new housing development, which you exit close to a bus stop where you can catch a bus back into town.

The city centre and Cambridge Railway Station are both around half a mile (1 km) from the start of the walk.

start	Junction of Trumpington Road and Brooklands Avenue
nearest postcode	CB2 7EB
finish	Trumpington Road (Anstey Way bus stop)
distance	4¼ miles / 6.9 km
time	2 hours
terrain	Paved, gravelled and earth paths which can be muddy. Shared cycle path. Kissing gates.

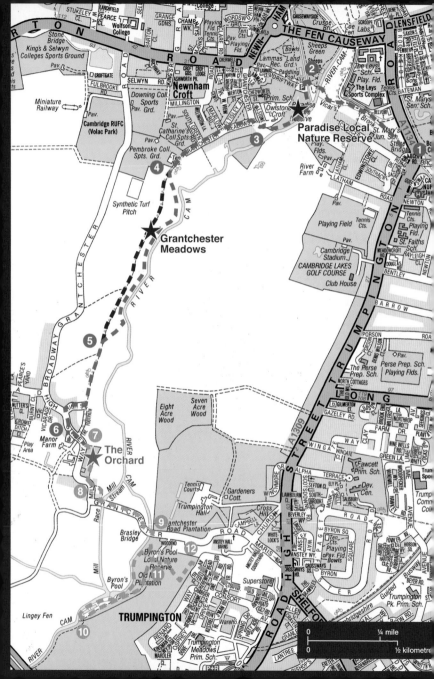

1 At the corner of Trumpington Road and Brooklands Avenue, and with your back to the main road, go onto the pedestrian and cycle tarmac path which parallels Vicar's Brook. This is signposted as a cycle route to Newnham, City Centre and West Cambridge. From spring to autumn, watch out for the cow pats – and occasionally the cattle, which graze on the grass. Keep left at path junctions until you reach the footbridge over the River Cam. As you cross it, look to your left to spot Hodson's Folly, built by a former college butler for his daughter.

2 A short distance further on, you cross a smaller bridge over a branch of the river, and turn left immediately afterwards, to skirt the edge of the car park. Go through the kissing gate into Paradise Local Nature Reserve ★. Follow the path through the green nature reserve as it skirts the river, until the path veers away and takes you through another gate onto a paved street.

3 Turn left after the gate. Follow the road as it bends to the right, and then turn left into the road called Grantchester Meadows, which is lined with Victorian houses. At the next road junction bear left, staying on Grantchester Meadows, which finally turns into a slightly pot-holed car park. Keep going straight, and enter a paved tree-lined path, at the end of which you go through another kissing gate. Don't use the cattle grid, which cyclists use.

4 The view now opens into vistas of the lovely Grantchester Meadows ★ which border the river. You have a choice: you can stay on the paved cycle path and carry straight on to Grantchester (following the directions from step 5), or you can go left and down to the river, taking the path which follows it. At times the riverside path may be quite muddy, but the views are a lovely recompense. After reaching the river, the path crosses three small bridges before it diverges. Take the right-hand fork here; the path makes its way away from the river and behind a row of trees before angling upwards to rejoin the paved cycle path.

5 Continue along the cycle path until you reach a gate on your right, leading to an unmetalled road followed by a paved road, with The Red Lion pub on the right. Go straight up to the main road, High Street, and turn left. Cross the road – it is rather bendy so take care when doing so.

6 The church straight ahead, parts of which date back to the 14th century or earlier, is recognizable from the television series *Grantchester*. There are a few steps down from its timbered entrance to the nave – a testament to the age of the church. After exploring the peaceful graveyard, exit by the same path. Turn right onto the road and cross it again carefully.

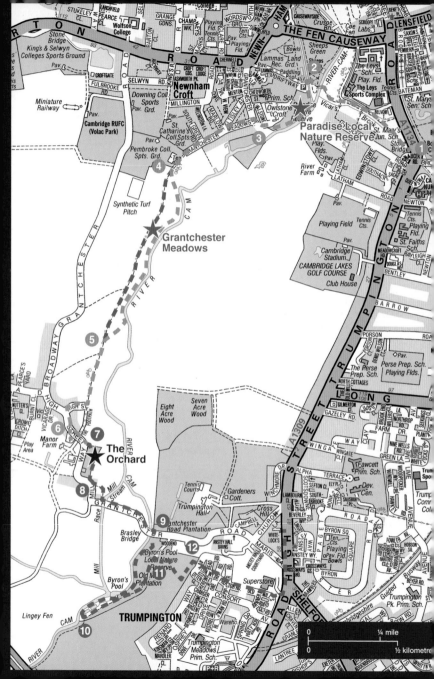

7 Walk on the pavement of Mill Way to the entrance to The Orchard Tea Garden ★ where you could stop for refreshment. The tea garden has been popular for decades among the students who have punted up to Grantchester after an all-night May Ball, and enjoyed breakfast there, relaxing in the orchard gardens after an exhausting night. Exit the Orchard through the car park and turn left back onto Mill Way. Pass the Old Vicarage, where the poet Rupert Brooke occasionally lived and which is the subject of his famous poem, 'The Old Vicarage, Grantchester'. Some interesting sculptures in its garden may be visible from the road.

8 Take the path on the left between high walls and an old red post box, which opens into an idyllic green beside the mill pond, with views into the Old Vicarage garden. Exit by the path to the road, turn left onto Grantchester Road and carefully cross the road. Immediately after the next bridge is the entrance to Byron's Pool Local Nature Reserve.

9 Entering the reserve, follow the path as it turns away from the river and leads to a picnic area and car park. Take the path to the right to cross the picnic area and then continue down to the river. The path winds through the woodland (and kissing gates), and views of the river show steps leading to green, hidden bathing areas where Lord Byron was reputed to have swum. Follow the path by the river past the modern weir (and nearby fish passageway).

10 You will reach a junction of paths, where the main path bends to the left; follow this path as it rises above the river, through green tree corridors near the edge of the reserve, and exit through a kissing gate to arrive back at the car park.

11 The path into the Trumpington Meadows Country Park is on the right almost immediately after exiting the Local Nature Reserve. Follow this gravelled path to a junction with other paths; turn right and then take the left fork, following the path to the next junction. Turn left and then take the next path to the right, which leads into the housing estate at the junction of Otter Close and Avalon Way.

12 Go straight ahead down Avalon Way, continuing straight as the road becomes Proctor Drive and then Old Mills Road. At the end of the road turn left and cross to the pavement of the main Hauxton Road. Follow this road to the left, crossing the supermarket entry and exit roads and continuing past Maris Lane, before reaching the bus stop beside a petrol station, from which there are frequent buses back into town.

Ⓐ🇿 walk nine

A Saucerful of Pink Floyd

The Victorian and Edwardian suburb that nurtured
the rock stars.

This short, circular walk explores the residential area in the southeast of the
city which is the spiritual home of the rock band Pink Floyd. Although the band
was formed in London during the 1960s, the main protagonists – Roger 'Syd'
Barrett, Roger Waters and Dave Gilmour – were all either born here or moved
here in early childhood.

As you visit the former homes and schools of the band members, you will
pass through the area between Hills Road and Cherry Hinton Road which was
developed for residential use as Cambridge expanded beyond the railway
station during late Victorian times. The main roads have different origins.
Hills Road follows the line of the Via Devana, a Roman road linking Colchester
with Cambridge. However, up until late Victorian times Cherry Hinton Road,
originally known as Long Drift, was no more than a farmland track.

You will walk along streets lined with houses built from the mid-1880s onwards.
Their different sizes – from substantial family homes to more modest terraced
cottages – show that the wealthy middle classes were living side by side
with those in humbler situations. You will also pass Homerton College, which
relocated to here from London in 1894, an Art Deco library and a model
cottage that is older than the road on which it stands.

The houses viewed on this walk are private residences – please consider the
residents as you view them.

start / finish	Cambridge Leisure Park, Cherry Hinton Road
nearest postcode	CB1 7AA
distance	1½ miles / 2.5 km
time	45 minutes
terrain	Pavements and shared cycle paths.

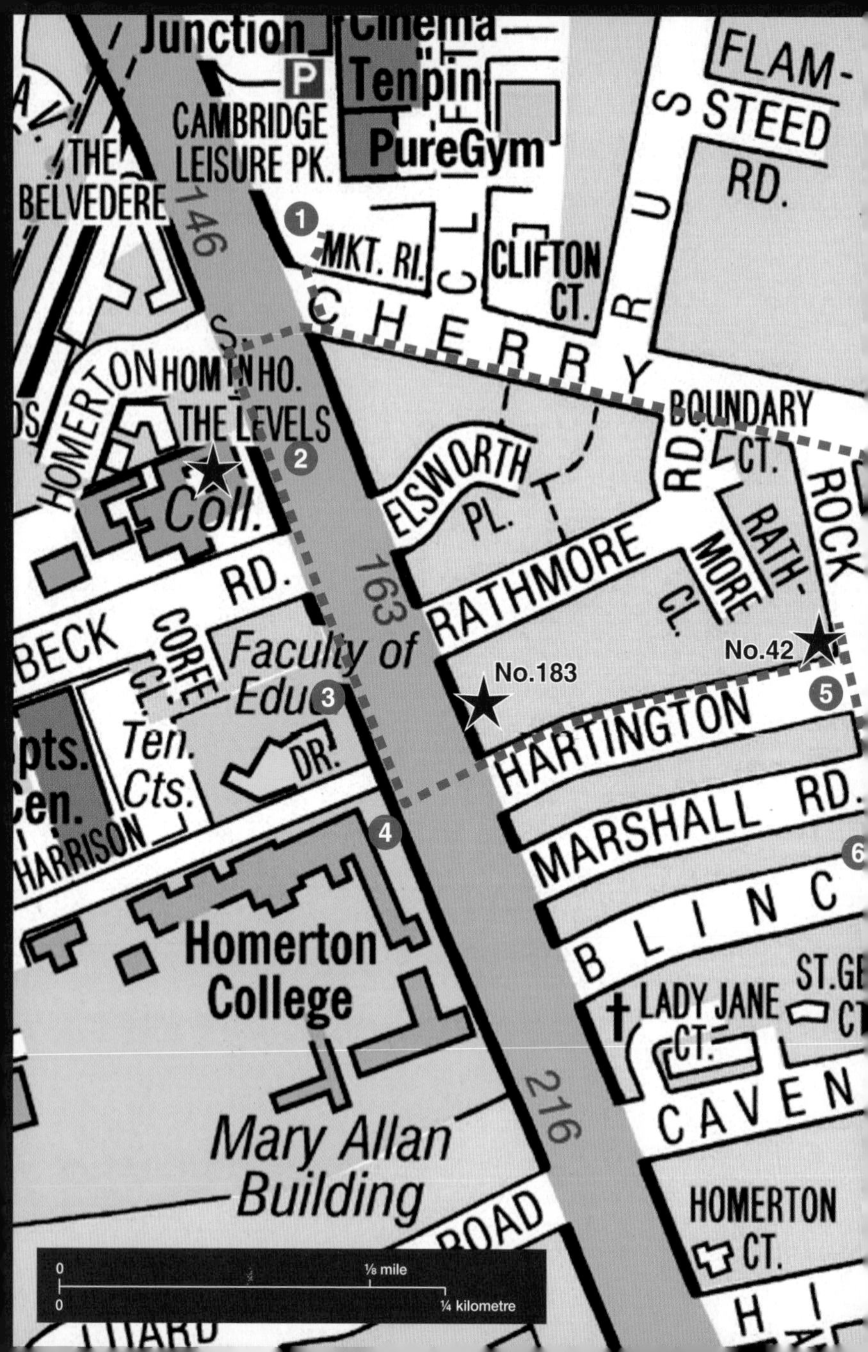

Junction
CAMBRIDGE
LEISURE PK.
P
THE
BELVEDERE
146

Cinema
Tenpin
PureGym

FLAM-
STEED
RD.

① MKT. RI.

CHERRY

CLIFTON
CT.

HOMERTON HOM'N HO.
THE LEVELS

② Coll.

HOMERTON

ELSWORTH
PL.

RD.

163

RATHMORE

BOUNDARY
CT.

RATH-
MORE
CL.

ROCK

RD.

CHERRY

CORFE
CL.

BECK

RD.

Faculty of
Edu ③

Ten.
Cts.

pts.
en.

HARRISON

DR.

④

No.183 ★

RATHMORE

HARTINGTON

No.42 ★
⑤

MARSHALL RD.

⑥

Homerton
College

B L I N C

LADY JANE
CT.

ST.GE
CT

Mary Allan
Building

216

ROAD

C A V E N

HOMERTON
CT.

HI

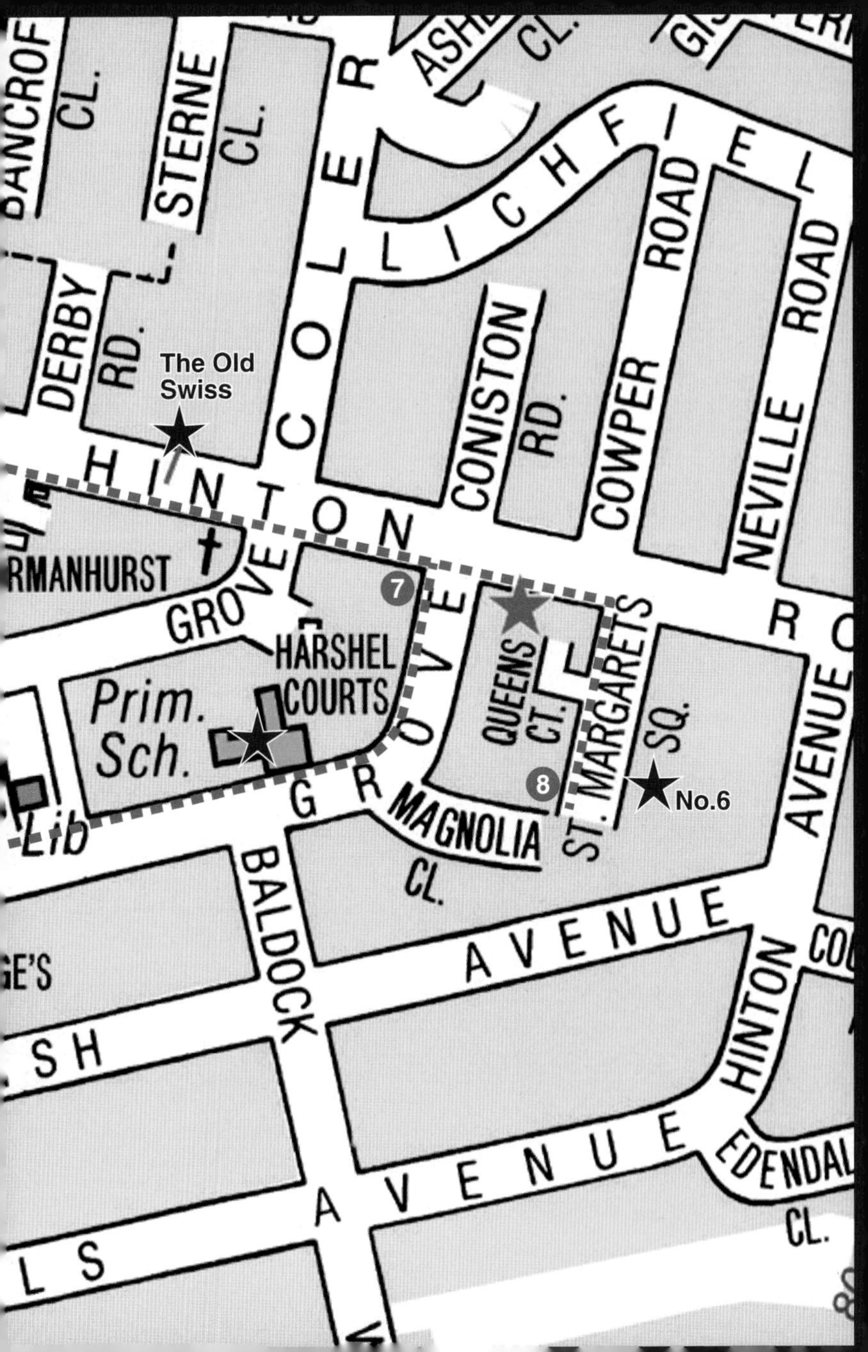

BANCROF CL.

STERNE CL.

ASH CL.

COLE

LICHFIE

Gl

DERBY RD.

The Old Swiss

CONISTON RD.

COWPER ROAD

NEVILLE ROAD

ROAD

HINTON

RMANHURST

GROVE

⑦

QUEENS CT.

HARSHEL COURTS

Prim. Sch.

GROVE

ST. MARGARETS

SQ.

⑧

No.6

Lib

MAGNOLIA CL.

BALDOCK

AVENUE

GE'S

SH

AVENUE

HINTON

CO

EDENDAL CL.

LS

1 Exit the Leisure Park onto Cherry Hinton Road and turn right. The Leisure Park is on the former site of the Cattle Market, which moved to this position in 1885; market day was on a Monday. Cross the road and bear right to the corner with Hills Road. Cross Hills Road and turn left.

2 After 200 yards (180 metres), Hills Road Sixth Form College ★ appears on the right; prior to 1974 this was the Cambridgeshire High School for Boys. From the edge of the drive, the old crest of the school is still clearly visible above the main doorway. In addition to Pink Floyd members Roger Waters and Syd Barrett, the 'County' educated an early band member, Bob Klose. Storm Thorgerson, responsible for many of the LP covers through his design company Hipgnosis, also attended here. It is generally recognized that the school provided some of the inspiration for the band's 1979 album, *The Wall*, which has sold more than 30 million copies. The recognizable lyrics of 'We don't need no education' and 'No dark sarcasm in the classroom' are testament to what seemed to have been an unhappy time for Waters. Continue along Hills Road.

3 After another 200 yards (180 metres), the entrance to Homerton College and Cambridge University's Faculty of Education appears on the right. Originally founded in London, Homerton came under the umbrella of Cambridge University in 2012, having previously served as a teacher training college. Although not generally open to the public, the 19th-century buildings, in the Gothic Revival style, can be seen from the road. Syd attended Saturday morning art classes there and The Pink Floyd Sound played at the summer party in 1965. When a teachers' training college, both Syd and Roger's mothers took in students as lodgers. The lodgers may have indirectly played a part in the creation of Pink Floyd's first hit 'Arnold Layne'. It is thought that Arnold Layne was based on a character who stole (and wore) young ladies' underwear from 'moonshine washing lines'.

4 Cross Hills Road at the pedestrian crossing and close by, on your left, is No. 183 ★. This was Syd Barrett's childhood and adolescent home from 1950 until 1964, when he left and went to Camberwell College of Arts in London. This was a meeting point for a 'shy and reclusive' Syd and many of his friends. When Syd returned in 1970, he lived in the basement and continued to do so until his mother sold the house and they both moved to St Margaret's Square. Take the next turning on the left into Hartington Grove.

5 After 300 yards (280 metres), turn left onto Rock Road. Number 42 ★ was the childhood and adolescent home of Roger Waters, seen by many as the leading figure in Pink Floyd throughout the 1970s. It is safe to assume that this was the scene of an incident described in the song 'When the Tigers Broke Free'. In the song, Waters recounts the time when, as a youth, he came across 'a scroll with gold leaf and all' in which 'kind old King George' had offered his condolences to Mrs Waters on the death of her husband. It had been 'hidden away … in a drawer of old photographs'. Roger Water's father was killed during the Second World War. Number 41, immediately opposite, was the home of Roger Water's first wife, Judy. Turn around and continue down Rock Road, passing the Art Deco-style public library, which opened in 1936, on the left.

6 Turn left onto Blinco Grove, where you will pass Morley Memorial Primary School ★ , attended by both Syd and Roger and where Roger's mother, Mary, taught – she had a reputation for being strict. The foundation stone was laid in 1899 and the school had close links with Homerton College as a practising school. Most of this area was built at the turn of the last century. Follow the road round as it bends to the left.

7 At the junction with Cherry Hinton Road, turn right. Immediately on the corner is The Rock pub; it is rumoured that in his later years an 'anonymous' Syd would use this as his local. Continue to the junction with St Margaret's Square, where you turn right and walk almost to the end. Number 6, St Margaret's Square ★ was where Syd lived with his mother in their later years, until her death, and then on his own until he died of cancer in 2006.

8 Retrace your steps to the junction with Cherry Hinton Road. Turn left and continue back along Cherry Hinton Road for just over half a mile (900 metres), passing The Rock on the left and, further along on the right, the redeveloped site of the former Swiss Laundry ★ . The laundry got its name from the Swiss finish it gave to table linen, but subsequently used the Swiss flag as its logo. Almost opposite the Swiss Laundry site, on the left-hand side, is No. 136, built in 1862 as a model cottage for the Vice Provost of King's College, Martin Thackeray. It stands at an angle to the other properties as it pre-dates Cherry Hinton Road itself. Continue to the junction with Hills Road and return to the starting point on the right.

A̅Z̅ walk ten

Concealed Chesterton

A village within the city.

Chesterton was a separate, wealthy village until the 1800s when it became subsumed into the city, and some hidden gems remain both in the old village and across the river. This walk takes you to past almshouses (built in 1801) to a 14th-century stand-alone tower, a residence owned at different times by an Italian abbey and a Cambridge college. Inside the nearby church is a stunning medieval 'Doom' wall-painting, while outside is a memorial to the daughter of anti-slavery campaigner Olaudah Equiano, also known as Gustavus Vassa, who had formerly been enslaved.

Crossing the river, and delving into the Victorian development on the site of a 12th-century abbey, you find the Cellarer's Chequer, one of the abbey's few surviving buildings. Returning to the river, you may spot a Dinky Door (a small public art installation), before retracing your steps past the fascinating Museum of Technology.

The route takes you to Stourbridge Common, the site of Europe's largest medieval fair, which took place annually from 1211 to 1933 and inspired John Bunyan's Vanity Fair. Crossing the river again, you return to the High Street, catching a glimpse of a sole remaining gas streetlight down a small side street, and passing a few remaining grand old houses.

A bus from the city centre will take you to the start of the walk.

start	High Street, Chesterton (Thrift's Walk bus stop)
nearest postcode	CB4 1NL
finish	High Street, Chesterton (Chesterton Road bus stop)
distance	2 miles / 3.2 km
time	1 hour
terrain	Pavements and paths. Steep bridge. Shared cycle paths.

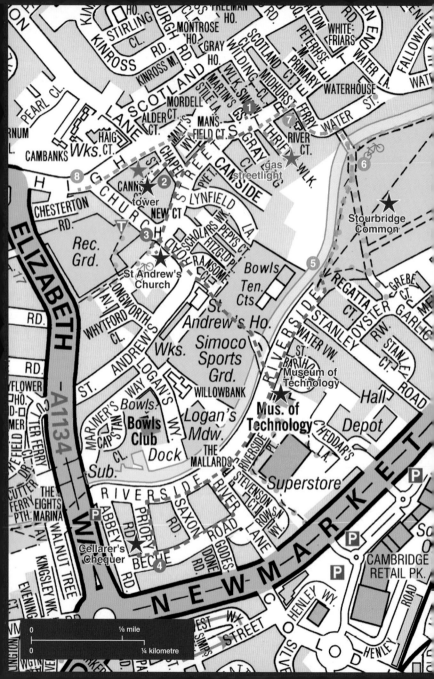

❶ From the bus stop, cross the road and turn right along the High Street. Turn left into Church Street, passing a large old house and its coach house, almshouses, Victorian terraces and more substantial homes. At the end of the street turn right into Chapel Street and take a short detour down the first (and only) driveway on the left into Chesterton Towers. The extraordinary medieval tower ★ is directly ahead of you, in the midst of 1960s blocks of flats.

❷ Turn back and exit Chesterton Towers. You will see the church hall next door to the left, now used as a nursery. Retrace your steps down Chapel Street and follow the road as it bends to the right and becomes Church Street again. At the T-junction, cross the road and take the short path to the Grade I listed St Andrew's Church ★ . On the outside wall is the memorial to Anna Maria Vassa, daughter of Equiano and a local woman, while inside the church is the 'Doom painting'. Enjoy the peace of the old graveyard.

❸ Returning to the road, turn right onto St Andrew's Road. Pass the Old Manor House on your right before turning left into the path signposted, for bicycles, to the City Centre, Station and Addenbrooke's. This leads to the interesting modern 'Equiano Bridge' over the River Cam. Exiting the bridge, carry straight on down Riverside before taking River Lane, the third road on the left. Walk up River Lane, taking the first right turn into Beche Road. Immediately after Priory Road (the second road on the right), stop to view the Cellarer's Chequer ★ , an extraordinary remnant of the Augustinian Priory of Barnwell.

❹ Go down Priory Road; at the T-junction look for a Dinky Door next to the post box. Turn right into Riverside, and carry straight on, passing the Museum of Technology ★ and its remarkable chimney, part of the Victorian sewage pumping station, on the right-hand side. It is often open for visiting. Continue straight along Riverside until you reach the entrance to Stourbridge Common ★ .

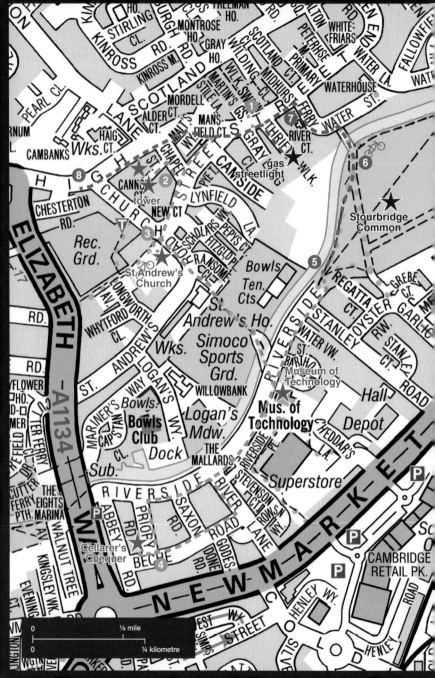

5 Go through the gate to the right rather than over the cattle grid which is used by cyclists. Carry straight on along the path by the river, avoiding the cow pats dropped by the unusual breeds of cows which graze the common from spring to autumn. Gardens are visible across the river, while swans, ducks and even herons can be seen, often avoiding rowing boats. At the fork in the path, veer to the right, away from the riverside.

6 After about 20 yards (18 metres), go through the pedestrian gate to the left of the cattle grid and over the steep Green Dragon Bridge, which gives lovely views up and down the river. On exiting the bridge turn left into Water Street, which bends to the right, becoming Ferry Lane. Roebuck House, on the bend, is one of the few grand old houses remaining in Chesterton. At the end of Ferry Lane turn left into the High Street.

7 Turn left again after 55 yards (50 metres) into Thrifts Walk to see ahead of you a single gas-fired streetlight ★. Retrace your steps and turn left, carrying on up the High Street for a further 450 yards (410 metres) to the end of the second Church Street on your left, where a couple more grand old houses can be seen.

8 Walk a little further to the next bus stop, to return to the city centre.

▲Z walk eleven

Future Cambridge

Eddington and West Cambridge.

While Cambridge is renowned for its beautiful old buildings in the historic centre, little is told about two modern University developments 2 miles (3.2 km) to the northwest of the city centre: Eddington and West Cambridge. Both are architecturally interesting developments, bordering countryside which provides a community amenity.

Eddington is primarily a residential area with the housing split between private houses for sale and social housing for university and college key workers. It is the largest development in the country being built to Level 5 of the Code for Sustainable Homes, with solar panels on all buildings, thick, highly insulated walls, rainwater harvesting and centralized production of heating.

Nearby, West Cambridge is a development of university buildings mainly for various science-oriented faculties, with a small amount of university housing. The architects and construction companies have worked together to consider not just the initial building costs, but also the costs of running the buildings over a long lifespan.

This walk can be extended to the village of Coton, whose pubs provide an opportunity for rest and refreshment. Buses from the city centre will take you on the short journey to the start of the walk in the centre of Eddington, or to the Madingley Road Park and Ride which is a short walk away.

start / finish	Eddington Avenue (Sainsbury's bus stop)
nearest postcode	CB3 1AA
distance	4½ miles / 7.5 km (+ optional 1½ miles / 2.3 km)
time	2 hours (+ optional 35 minutes)
terrain	Pavements, paved and gravelled paths. Shared cycle paths. Steps (optional). Steep climb on the optional extension.

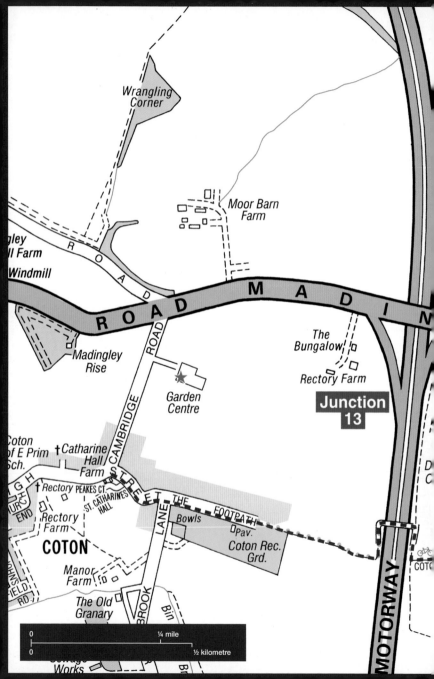

Wrangling Corner

Moor Barn Farm

ngley
ll Farm

Windmill

R O A D

R O A D   M A D I N

The Bungalow

Rectory Farm

Junction 13

Madingley Rise

Garden Centre

Coton
of E Prim
Sch.

† Catharine
Hall
Farm

† Rectory PEAKES CT.

ST. CATHARINES
HALL

Rectory
Farm

COTON

Manor
Farm

The Old
Granary

H
I
G
H

URCH

END

FIELD
RD.

CAMBRIDGE   STREET

LANE

BROOK

Bin

THE   FOOTPATH

Bowls

Pav.

Coton Rec.
Grd.

MOTORWAY

COTO

ewage
Works

| 0 | | ¼ mile |
| 0 | | ½ kilometre |

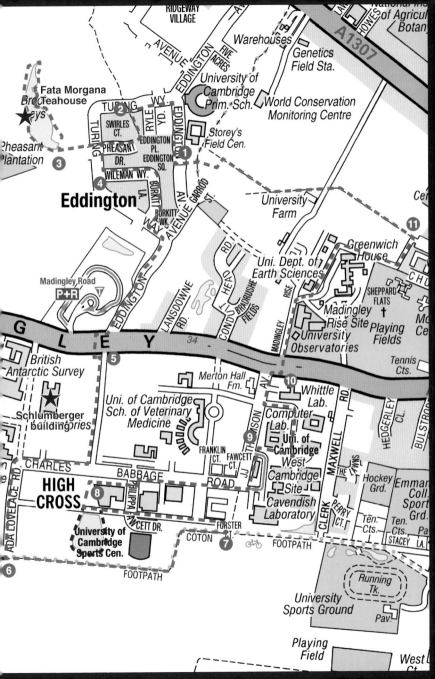

RIDGEWAY VILLAGE

National Ins. of Agricul. Botan...

A1307

Warehouses

Genetics Field Sta.

AVENUE

FIVE ACRES

EDDINGTON

University of Cambridge Prim. Sch.

World Conservation Monitoring Centre

Fata Morgana Bro Teahouse ays

TURING WY.

2

SWIRLES CT.

RYLE WY.

EDDINGTON

Storey's Field Cen.

Pheasant Plantation

3

TURING

PHEASANT DR.

EDDINGTON PL.

EDDINGTON SQ.

1

EDDINGTON

4

WILEMAN WY.

BURKITT LA.

AVENUE

GARROD ST.

University Farm

Ce...

11

Eddington

BURKITT WK.

EDDINGTON WAY

RD.

HEA...

RISE

Uni. Dept. of Earth Sciences

Greenwich House

CH...

Madingley Road P+R

LANSDOWNE RD.

COND

BRADRUSHE FIELDS

MADINGLEY

SHEPPARD FLATS

Madingley Risé Site

Mo Ce...

G

L

E

Y

34

University Observatories

Playing Fields

British Antarctic Survey

5

Merton Hall Fm.

AV.

10

Whittle Lab.

RD.

Tennis Cts.

HEDGERLEY CT.

BULSTRO...

Schlumberger buildingsories

Uni. of Cambridge Sch. of Veterinary Medicine

THOMSON

Computer Lab.

Uni. of Cambridge West Cambridge Site

MAXWELL RD.

THE AWNS

Hockey Grd.

Emma Coll. Sport Grd.

CHARLES

FRANKLIN CT.

FAWCETT CT.

9

ADA LOVELACE RD.

HIGH CROSS

8

PHILIPPA

BABBAGE ROAD

FAWCETT DR.

Cavendish Laboratory

CLERK

PERRY CT.

Tén: Cts.

Ten. Cts. STACEY LA.

Pa...

University of Cambridge Sports Cen.

FORSTER CT.

COTON

7

FOOTPATH

6

FOOTPATH

Running Tk.

University Sports Ground

Pav.

Playing Field

West ...

1 From the bus stop on Eddington Avenue, walk north up the road past the hotel and the University of Cambridge Primary School. Take Turing Way – the first road left – named after Kings College and Bletchley Park alumnus Alan Turing. Pass three blocks of flats on your right and a large oak tree, reputed to be more than 500 years old, and turn sharp left into the tree-lined Ridge Way.

2 In the building on your right, note the windows with ventilation panels to the side, and the deep-set windows in the building to your left; both features are intended to minimize temperature variations in the rooms. At the end of the road turn right, signposted to Brook Leys; go past Girton College's Swirles Court and down Pheasant Drive, noting the water soakaway 'moat' to your right.

3 Take a dogleg straight on down a gravel path to the lake. Walk straight on and around the small lake, with earthen hills by its side minimizing the noise from the nearby motorway. Detour via the *Fata Morgana Teahouse* installation ★, then round the top of the lake, and on the return take the right fork down along the edge of the lake. On rejoining the main path, turn right and return to the starting point at the south of the lake. Go left, and at Turing Way turn right.

4 Cross the road and take the first left (Wileman Way), from where you can catch glimpses of gardens behind the buildings. At the top you can detour into the Market Square (look for the rainwater harvesting drains) before turning right down Burkitt Lane, passing the central Energy Centre. On rejoining Turing Way turn left, and at the junction cross Turing Way again, continuing down Eddington Avenue, past the Park and Ride, to the traffic lights at Madingley Road.

5 Cross Madingley Road at the traffic lights and carry straight on, noting the tent-like Schlumberger building ★ on your right. At the T-junction turn right into Charles Babbage Road and at the next T-junction turn left into Ada Lovelace Road, named after the woman who worked with Babbage on his difference and analytic engines during the 19th century. At the end of the road is the Coton Footpath.

6 If you would like to extend your walk to the village of Coton, turn right along the Coton Footpath and carry straight on for three-quarters of a mile (1.15 km). The path goes over the motorway and to Coton, where you can explore the village and its pubs. You then need to retrace your steps back to the junction of the footpath with Ada Lovelace Road and continue straight ahead along the footpath. If you don't go to Coton, turn left at this junction and follow the tree-lined Coton Footpath along the edge of fields. Directly ahead in the distance you can see the tower of the University Library and a few church spires through the trees. The footpath bends left and then right before reaching a sharp left entrance to the West Cambridge site.

7 Follow the path going left, onto the wide road called Canal Path, past some university residence buildings and the Department of Chemical Engineering and Biotechnology until you reach West Cambridge Lake on your left, which you can walk round if you choose (530 yards / 500 metres). Turn right and climb the steps to the top of the grass seating area where, weather permitting, you can sit and look over the lake and the fields beyond.

8 Turn right along the pavement past the Department of Materials Science and Metallurgy, then turn left into Philippa Fawcett Drive, named after the woman who got the top first-class honours in maths in the University in 1890, but, as a woman, could not be awarded a degree. At the junction, turn right into Charles Babbage Road; at the main junction turn left into JJ Thomson Avenue.

9 After 130 yards (120 metres), turn right just after the Maxwell Centre and walk down The Green, a footpath leading past the Department of Computer Science and Technology. When you come to the road, turn left and follow it past the Electrical Engineering Division after which it bends left to rejoin JJ Thomson Avenue. Turn right along JJ Thomson Avenue, and walk past the Whittle Laboratory, named after the inventor of the jet engine, to Madingley Road.

10 Cross Madingley Road at the traffic lights and take a dogleg straight on into Madingley Rise, on the left edge of the Observatory buildings. Take the right fork in the road and, after 80 yards (70 metres), take the path to the left signposted as the cycleway to Storey's Way. Carry straight on; the tree-lined path bends to the right, exits the woodland and turns left among buildings.

11 At the next junction turn left, signposted to Storey's Field Centre, and Superstore. Continue straight along the Ridgeway; it bends left shortly before crossing a small road. Shortly after that, take a right fork gravelled path marked as for pedestrians. Just before the pedestrian path turns right, take a left turn to rejoin the cycleway. Turn right onto the Ridgeway and go past the Storey's Centre. The bus stop for the bus back into town is immediately ahead of you.

Az walk twelve

Follow the Bumps

The route of the rowing races along the River Cam.

The Bumps are rowing races for coxed Eights, peculiar to Cambridge (and Oxford), which evolved because the river is too narrow for traditional racing. Seventeen boats start one-and-a-half boat lengths apart and race the 2-mile (3.2-km) course to catch the boat ahead. Upon 'bumping', both boats retire from the race and the following day switch places for the start. Bumps races take place over a period of four days, three or four times a year.

This normally peaceful and bucolic walk takes you down the towpath next to the river where, as well as lovely riverside scenery you will see swans, ducks and maybe a heron or two. In places, longboats are moored at the riverside, and occasionally summer passenger boats conduct river tours. Rowers may be practising; the swans seem adept at avoiding their blades.

At Baits Bite Lock you cross the river and follow a rural path back up to your starting point, passing through woodland, fields and hedged paths. The walk takes in the lovely old village of Fen Ditton, where you might stop for refreshment at one of its pubs, or explore the towered church which dates from the 12th century. A route across Ditton's riverside meadows and Stourbridge Common, site of the largest medieval fair in Europe, takes you to the end of the walk.

A bus from the city centre will take you to the start of the walk.

start / finish	High Street, Chesterton (Thrift's Walk bus stop)
nearest postcode	CB4 1NW
distance	4¾ miles / 7.6 km
time	2 hours
terrain	Paved roads, gravel and dirt paths, which can be muddy. Shared cycle paths. Steep bridge, steps and kissing gates.

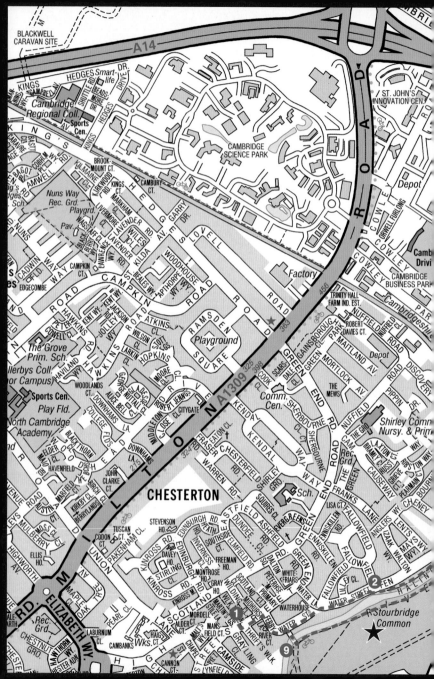

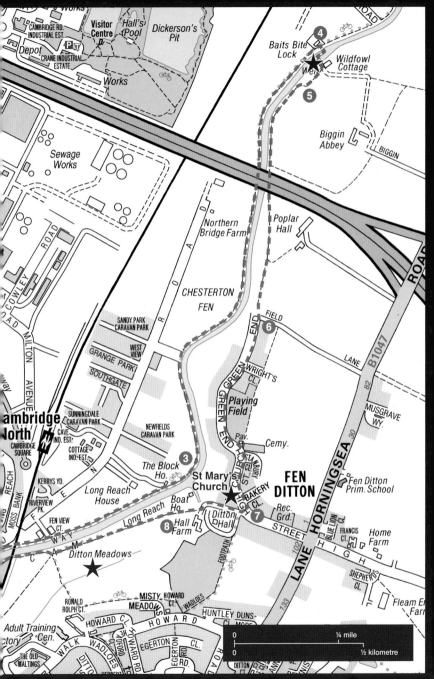

1 From the bus stop, cross the road and turn left along the High Street for 60 yards (55 metres). Turn right into Ferry Lane which bends left, becoming Water Street. At the end of the street go through the bollards and turn right. Walk past a few houses to a small car park; turn into it and go straight ahead through the bollards (known as 'Peter's Posts'), and on to the path by the river.

2 You are now on the gravelled towpath, also known as Haling Way, on which you will walk 1¾ miles (2.9 km) to reach Baits Bite Lock. Beware of cyclists throughout this joint pedestrian and bicycle path, particularly at the short tarmac section, after 400 yards (365 metres), where speeding bicycles pass under the railway and the pedestrian/cycle bridges over the river. Walk on beside the straight river section known as Long Reach.

3 As the river bends to the left, there are some lovely houses bordering the other side of the river, as well as the gardens of a riverside pub. As the river winds onward, you can see further away some houses of the village of Fen Ditton, after which the walk becomes more rural, with trees overhanging the river. Walk along the curves of the river and under the bridge carrying the busy A14 road.

4 After a further 700 yards (640 metres) you reach Baits Bite Lock ★, where you might see a longboat navigating the river drop. Climb up and down the steps to cross the lock, and then take the bridge over the weir to reach the other riverbank. Follow the path for a few paces; where it diverges take the right fork at the edge of the field, passing behind the wooden hoarding.

5 From this point onwards, the path can become quite muddy. It forms a woodland tunnel for 230 yards (210 metres) before reaching the first of the kissing gates. After a similar distance you pass under the unlovely concrete A14 bridge, before a kissing gate, directly ahead of you, leads into a path across fields. Another kissing gate takes you to a hedge-lined path which passes next to an isolated house, and over a small crest to yet another kissing gate.

6 After a few steps, you enter the paved road passing through the historic village of Fen Ditton. Along this road, evocatively named Green End, are many old houses. A short driveway runs backwards to a pub with riverside gardens, while further along the road (now named Church Street) you pass the beautiful Old Rectory before reaching an old pub across from St Mary's Church ★. You may wish to explore the church, which dates to the 12th century.

7 Exiting the church, turn right down the High Street (although you might first like to explore the old High Street in the other direction). Your route carries on down the short hill to where the tarmac turns into stones. The path bends to the left and reaches a final kissing gate, through which you reach the wide green Ditton Meadows ★ which border the river.

8 Walk along the river edge, through an open wide gate and onwards, eventually crossing a small wooden bridge over a creek and reaching a tarmac path. Go through the gate next to the cattle grid (used by cyclists) and on under the bridges. Follow the tarmac path near the river across Stourbridge Common ★ , the site of the largest medieval fair in Europe, which took place annually from 1211 to 1933 and inspired John Bunyan's Vanity Fair. Isaac Newton probably bought his glass prism there, which he used to develop his theory on the visible spectrum of light.

9 After 800 yards (730 metres) you reach a junction of paths; turn right and go through the pedestrian gate to the left of the cattle grid and over the steep Green Dragon Bridge which gives lovely views up and down the river. You could stop for a well-deserved refreshment at the pub opposite the exit to the bridge before turning left along Water Street and up Ferry Lane to the High Street. Turn left and walk about 100 yards (90 metres) to the bus stop for the bus back into town. If you wish to discover the hidden gems of Chesterton, you could follow walk ten, which starts here.

A͞Z walk thirteen

A Walk with Nature

Milton Country Park and the River Cam.

Three miles (4.8 km) to the northeast of the city centre, Milton Country Park opened in 1993 on the site of former gravel pits that had provided sand and gravel as building materials for a growing Cambridge between 1930 and 1960. However, the first material taken from the site was clay, in much smaller quantities, by Romano-British potters about 1,800 years previously. Today, it is a 95-acre park of varied natural habitat interlaced with over 3 miles (5 km) of paths. The park includes a Visitor Centre with café, play areas, viewing platforms and lakes. Toilet facilities are available.

Although a popular place with local people, hosting events such as park runs and open water swimming, it also offers peace and quiet. There are places to stop and rest, where the views over the old gravel pits, now lakes, offer a chance to see nature in its many forms.

From the start, the route takes you into the village of Milton, with a short walk along its High Street and into the side entrance of the Country Park, where you can explore the paths and trails at leisure. Leaving on the Fen Road, a short walk takes you through open countryside to the River Cam and Baits Bite Lock, before you retrace your steps back through Milton.

Milton Park and Ride is accessible by a short bus journey from Cambridge centre. Parking is also available free of charge.

start / finish	Milton Park and Ride, Butt Lane, Milton
nearest postcode	CB24 6ZH
distance	4¼ miles / 6.7 km
time	2 hours
terrain	Mainly paved roads and paths. Shared cycle paths and one steep bridge. Steps (optional). The Country Park trails may be muddy in places..

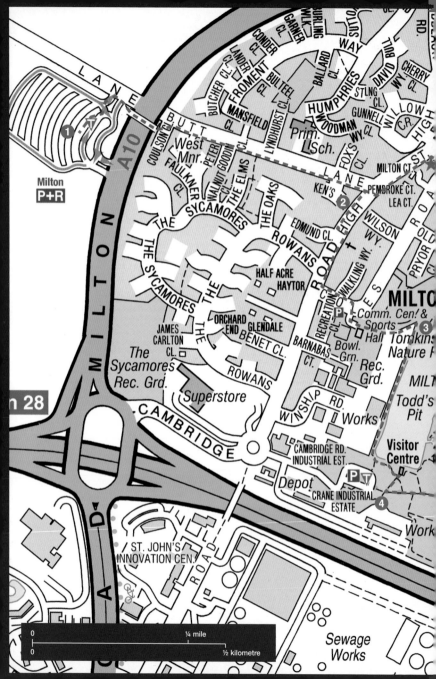

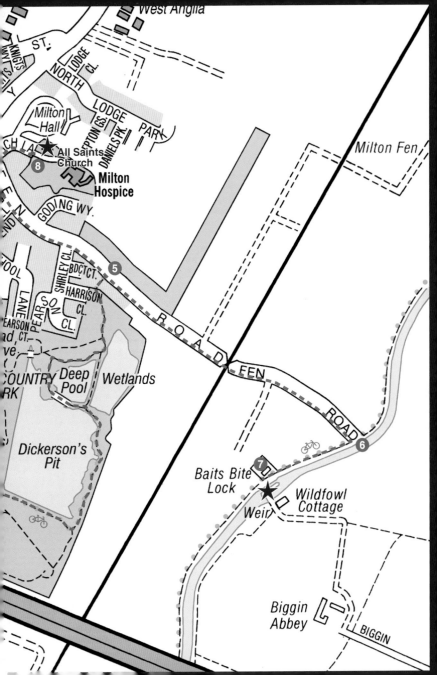

1 Exit the Park and Ride site at the Butt Lane entrance and turn right towards the A10. Within a few yards/metres the pedestrian/cycle bridge is on the right, which is used to cross the A10 and rejoin Butt Lane the other side. Walk down the length of Butt Lane for a quarter of a mile (550 metres) to Milton High Street. Milton is situated on 'high ground' away from the river and settlements can be traced back to Roman times. However much of the architecture on view is relatively modern, reflecting its growth during the second half of the 20th century.

2 Turn right along Milton High Street, which becomes Cambridge Road, and use the pedestrian crossing just after a small row of shops to cross over. Turn left into Coles Road and after 100 yards (90 metres), where the road bends sharply to the left, turn right into the village complex containing a doctor's surgery, village hall, pre-school and playing fields. Follow the path between the doctor's surgery and Community Centre, and cross the playing field keeping to the left.

3 At a small gate, enter Milton Country Park ★ and turn right, taking the path along the side of Todd's Pit. Todd's Pit is a relatively small and shallow freshwater lake created following the extraction of sands and gravel during the 20th century. Today it is popular with fishermen, particularly those looking for carp. After 300 yards (250 metres) the path leads to an area with a café, playgrounds and a sensory garden. Continue for a short distance until it meets with the main path. This may be a place to stop and take advantage of the facilities.

4 Turn left and take the path, passing a playground, along the top of Dickerson's Pit; the path turns left around the side of the lake. Dickerson's Pit was again created by the extraction of sands and gravel. During winter it is home to many migratory birds. Keep left, crossing two small bridges, with Dickerson's Pit on the left and Deep Pool on the right. Keeping Deep Pool on your right, follow the path to the top of Deep Pool before turning left, staying on the path, and exiting the Country Park at Fen Road.

5 Turn right on Fen Road and continue for half a mile (800 metres), crossing the Cambridge–Ely railway line (opened in 1845). You will pass open fields and drainage ditches (drains); this is one of the oldest routes in Milton village, dating from at least the 13th century. The drains meet the river at a sluice gate and there are often ducks, geese and swans in residence looking for a free meal. The left-hand path leads along the river to Clayhithe and the banks are often occupied by local fishermen and some houseboats.

6 Turn right along the River Cam for 250 yards (200 metres), until reaching Baits Bite Lock ★. (It is here that this walk meets walk twelve.) Baits Bite Lock was built in the early 1700s as the river was in poor condition and barely navigable. The lockkeeper's cottage is still in evidence, although today it is redundant as the lock is electronically controlled. It is worth taking a little time to examine the area and the river, which can be seen to best advantage by climbing the steps to the bridge over the weir.

7 Return along the same route, turning left away from the river at Fen Road, and continue the full length of Fen Road, passing the entrance to the Country Park on the left. This is the older part of Milton, evidenced by old and sometimes thatched or tiled houses. Just before the junction with the High Street on the right-hand side and after the Brewers Inn is Church Lane. This is the old centre of the village, and Church Lane will take you to All Saints Church ★.

8 Retrace your steps back along Church Lane, turning right onto Fen Road, and at Milton High Street turn left for 220 yards (200 metres) until you reach Butt Lane on the right-hand side. Walk the full length of Butt Lane until you reach the cycle/pedestrian bridge over the A10. Upon crossing the bridge you will find yourself back at the start point.

A⧸Z walk fourteen

Tudors and Topiary

Madingley Hall and Cambridge American Cemetery.

This is a gem of a short walk. It is full of variety and discovery, centring around a Tudor mansion, Madingley Hall, within an 18th-century Capability Brown landscape. There are hidden features such as topiary gardens, a pets' cemetery and some stone carved angels which survived the Puritan iconoclast, William Dowsing.

The walk begins with a door in a wall, behind which are beds of medicinal herbs, alpines and a rose pergola. A grand gateway, brought from the Cambridge Old Schools building, enriches the impressive 16th-century house. Queen Victoria's son, Edward, stayed here when he studied at Cambridge University. It is said that this is where his father, Prince Albert, caught the chill which led to his death.

Around Madingley Hall there are hidden topiary gardens, a croquet lawn and a handsome avenue. The perimeter path winds through woodland, filled with bulbs in the spring. A lake with a bridge provide a focal point. A visit to the village church is rewarding. Back at the Hall there are stables to be viewed, and a delightful café with pictures of many great women and men associated with Cambridge University. The Hall and the estate are run by the University and used as a continuing education and conference centre.

The walk can be extended by a visit to the nearby Cambridge American Cemetery.

start / finish	Madingley Hall car park, Madingley
nearest postcode	CB23 8AQ
distance	1 mile / 1.7 km
time	30 minutes (+ optional 30 minutes to American Cemetery)
terrain	Paved roads and firm paths. Steps.

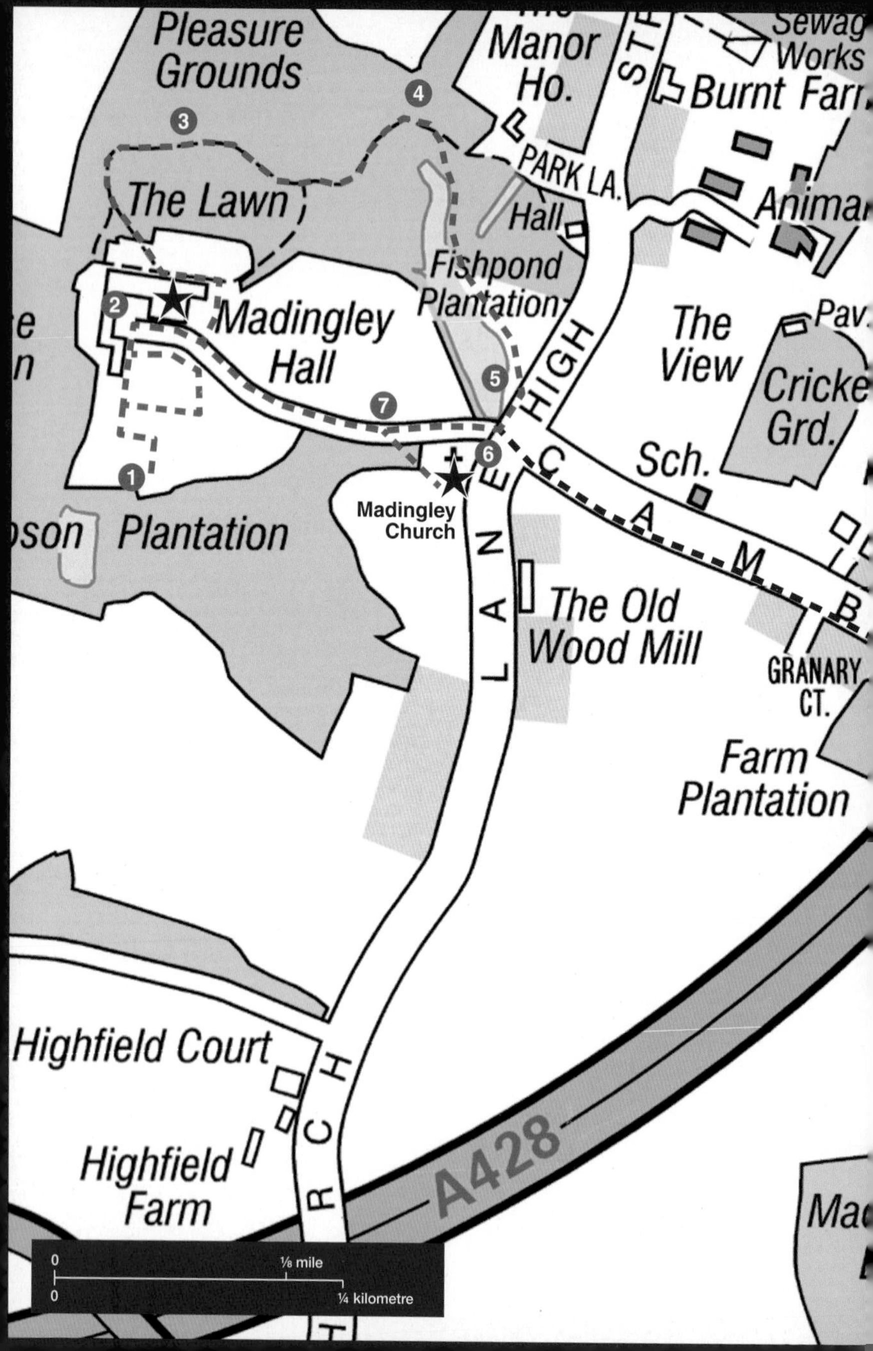

Pleasure
Grounds

The
Manor
Ho.

STR

Sewag
Works

Burnt Farr

③

The Lawn

④

PARK LA.

Animar

Hall

Fishpond
Plantation

⑤

The
View

Pav.

Cricke
Grd.

②

★ Madingley Hall

e
n

⑦

⑥

HIGH

Sch.

GRANARY
CT.

①

oson

Plantation

★ Madingley Church

LANE

CHURCH

The Old
Wood Mill

C A M B

Farm
Plantation

Highfield Court

Highfield
Farm

A428

Mad

| 0 | | ⅛ mile |
| 0 | | ¼ kilometre |

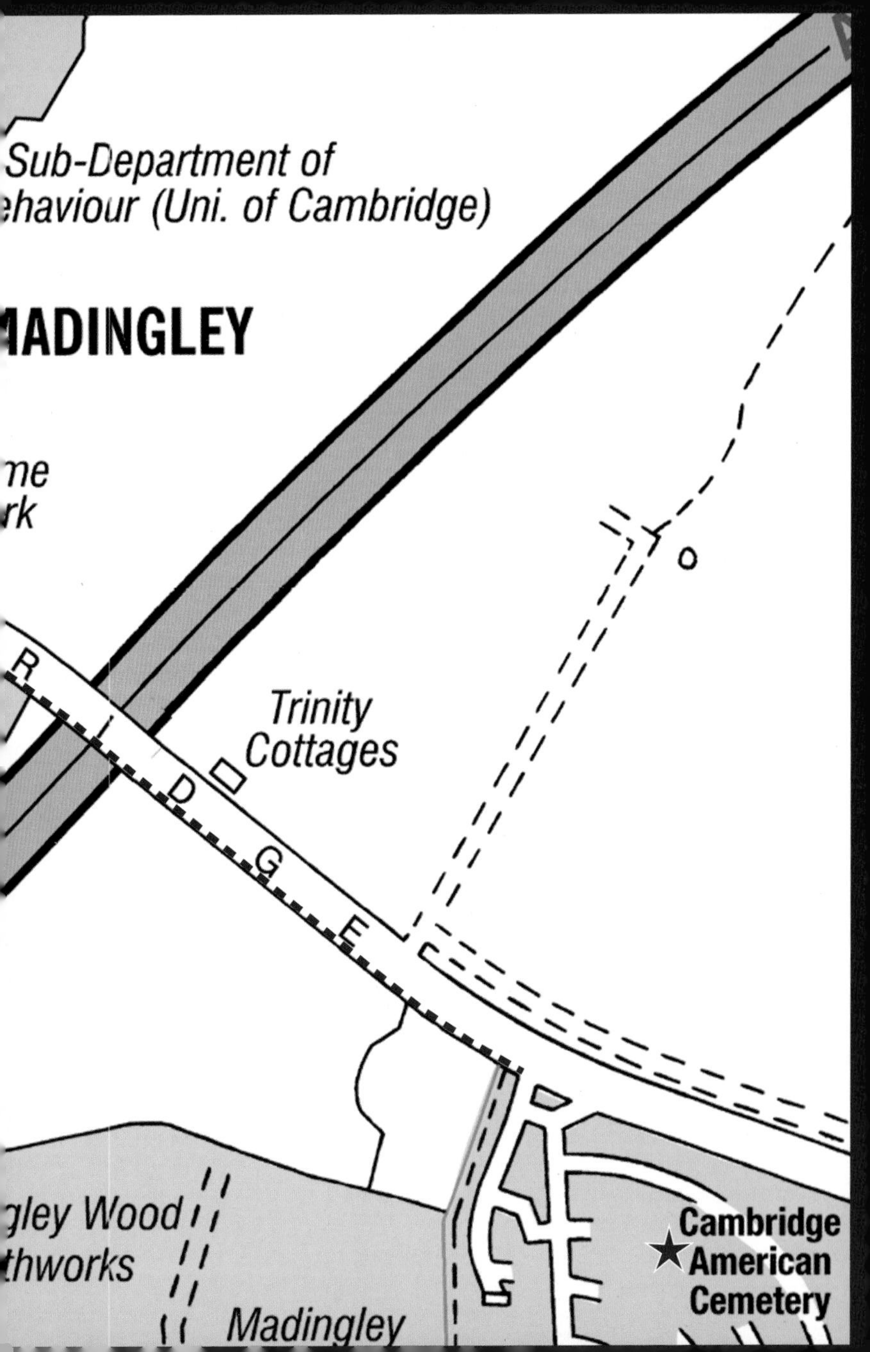

Sub-Department of
ehaviour (Uni. of Cambridge)

MADINGLEY

ne
rk

R

Trinity
Cottages

D

G

E

gley Wood
thworks

Madingley

Cambridge
★**American**
Cemetery

1 Start in the car park and enter a door in the wall facing the grand Madingley Hall ★. Turn right, and walk three sides of a beautiful walled garden, established in the 18th century. It is laid out with a sense of hidden rooms, and you may want to explore some of the paths, or the tunnel of hazel trees. Leave through a white door and go down some steps.

2 Turn right and go through a medieval archway. Turn left and walk in front of the magnificent Grade I listed Tudor mansion. Beyond the forecourt is a small terrace with topiary and a pond. Take the small wooden gate, go through this garden, and continue to the left, round the Hall. About two-thirds of the way along the gravelled path, turn right at a spiral topiary. At a T-junction, turn right and follow the perimeter fence.

3 At the end of a yew avenue, go through a gate on your left. Enter the Wilderness Grove – a feature of grand houses that was popular in the time of Jane Austen. Walk through pretty woodland, full of bulbs in the springtime. Tucked away to the left of the path are some small gravestones, marking the burial place of beloved pets from the big house.

4 Cross a little bridge over a ditch. Turn right and walk around a lake (on the side furthest from the Hall) until you get close to an ornamental bridge (it doesn't actually go across the water – it was built as an aesthetic feature!). The path ends just outside the park.

5 Turn right and continue beside the road for a few yards until you reach the main gates to the Hall, by the roundabout. If you wish to extend the walk to include the American Cemetery ★, stand with your back to the gates and take the road in front of you, Cambridge Road. It's about a 15-minute walk to the back entrance of the cemetery, a moving memorial to the American forces who died during the Second World War. Afterward, retrace your steps to the main gates to the Hall.

6 Walk through the main gates to the Hall and along the entrance track. Branch off to the left to visit the parish church ★. When the park was landscaped in the 18th century, several houses were knocked down to give the impression that the church was a part of the estate. There is much to enjoy inside, including a fine font, some fragments of Tudor glass and carved angels, which were deliberately damaged during the English Civil War.

7 Leave the church, and rejoin the main track, turning left and returning to the Hall. You may wish to spend some time looking at the stable block and ornamental pond. There are facilities such as toilets, and a bar/restaurant. There are even B&B rooms. Complete the walk by returning through the wooden gate to the walled garden. Go straight ahead to the far door to the car park, to return to the start point.

ᴀ𝐳 walk fifteen

The Fen Edge Village

Landbeach, a Roman road and a wildlife haven.

The village of Landbeach lies just off the Mere Way, a Roman road that linked Cambridge with the Fens, part of which you will follow on this walk. The Fens are a low-lying area of natural marshland extending north from Cambridge as far as Lincoln, and east to Norfolk and Suffolk. Much of the marsh has been drained, leaving level, fertile land that is ideal for agriculture. Landbeach is classed as a Fen Edge village and lies 5 miles (8 km) northeast of the city centre.

The Mere Way takes you the heart of the village, where a stroll around will unveil All Saints' Church, with stonework dating to the Norman Conquest and links to Corpus Christi College, Cambridge. The East window appears to show Lady Margaret Beaufort, mother of King Henry VII and grandmother of Henry VIII.

The route detours to the Tithe Barn before returning to the Mere Way, and the start point, via Worts Meadow. Here you will pass through a former medieval settlement site, with its surviving homestead moat and fishpond. This is thought to be the old manor of Bray. The trail then leads into Bourne Wood, filled with native species of trees, ponds and wildlife.

The start and finish point of this walk, Milton Park and Ride, is accessible by a short bus journey from Cambridge centre. Parking is also available free of charge.

start / finish	Milton Park and Ride, Butt Lane, Milton
nearest postcode	CB24 6ZH
distance	4½ miles / 7 km
time	2 hours
terrain	Paved paths, grass track and bridleway, which can be muddy. Shared cycle paths and narrow roads without pavements.

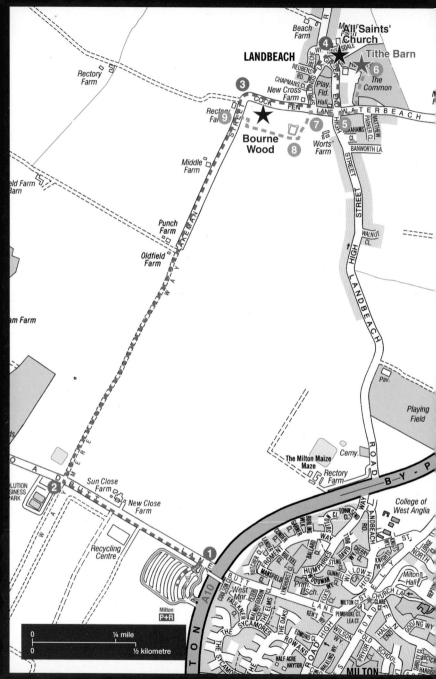

1 Exit the Park and Ride site at the Butt Lane entrance and turn left, away from the A10 for a distance of half a mile (900 metres), towards the villages of Histon and Impington. You pass the Recycling Centre on the left and Sunclose Farm on the right. Although very quiet, the path is shared by both pedestrians and cyclists.

2 Turn right along the Mere Way. The first half mile (1 km) is a wide, tree-lined bridleway going past Sunclose Farm on the right and fields on the left. The terrain is uneven but flat and in wet weather the puddles are usually easily negotiable. The bridleway turns into a metalled road, becoming Akeman Street, passing working farms on the left and open fields on the right. Depending on the time of day, and time of year, there is the opportunity to view a variety of wildlife.

3 After 1¼ miles (2 km), the road takes a sharp right, becoming Cock Fen Lane, and passes Bourne Wood and Worts Meadows on the right-hand side. At Spaldings Lane, turn left. You will notice a small gate on the right, which gives access to the recreation ground and children's play area where there are picnic tables and seating available. Continue along Spaldings Lane, passing the recreation ground on your right, before merging with Green End to the right.

4 All Saints' Church ★ is clearly visible and is accessible through the gate. The countryside graveyard contains the graves of many Landbeach families and also, at the rear of the church, that of Robert Masters, a former Master of Corpus Christi College in Cambridge. There are a number of links to the College, evidence of Norman stonework, interesting misericords and an East window assumed to depict Lady Margaret Beaufort. A short guidebook is normally available. In June and July, the church is usually visited by swifts, nesting in the tower, and these can be viewed in the church through a video link. Leaving the church, turn left along Green End passing the Rectory behind its high wall, Copt Hall now divided into three small cottages, and the Old School, before reaching the crossroads.

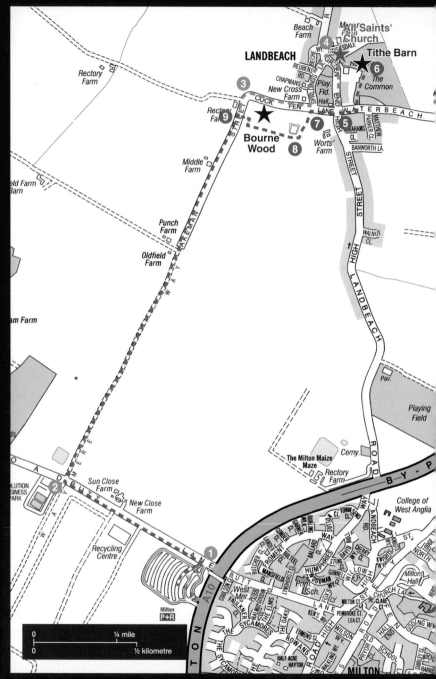

5 Turn left onto Waterbeach Road, passing local allotments on the left. After approximately 180 yards (150 metres), on the left roughly opposite Far View Villa, is the path leading to the Tithe Barn ★ , one of only a handful in the county. Tithe barns were built in the days when peasants gave a 'tithe' or tenth of their crops to the Church. There has been a tithe barn on this site for at least 650 years, and whilst there is some dispute over its age, the present structure is believed to be approximately 500 years old. The barn, last thatched in 2019 in reed, is viewable from the outside. Look out over common land and see evidence of an older landscape with its ditches leading to old commercial waterways.

6 Retrace your steps to the crossroads at the High Street and go straight across onto Cock Fen Lane, passing the Village Hall on the right. If signs show the Village Hall to be open, then it may be possible to purchase a drink. After 100 yards (90 metres), the entrance to Worts Meadow is on the left-hand side opposite Spaldings Lane; an information board is at the entrance.

7 Turn into Worts Meadow, a Scheduled Monument under the Ancient Monuments and Archaeological Areas Act 1979, deemed to be of the highest quality and of national importance. Follow the track across Worts Meadow to the moat, passing the pond on the left. The

moat belongs to the old manor of Bray, mentioned in the Domesday Book. The earthworks around the site indicate that smaller houses and other structures surrounded the manor house, but these appear to have been abandoned in the 14th century.

8 Go through the gate and follow the track on the left side of the field, through another gate and into Bourne Wood ★ . The wood contains predominantly native species and, since being planted in 1992, has developed well. There are four ponds on the site which are the most important areas for wildlife. Keep going straight along the track for 200 yards (180 metres). It then bends to the right and comes to a gate on the left, leading onto Akeman Street. Ponds have been dug to encourage great crested newts and other tracks are available for exploration – it is difficult to get lost! You might choose to sit on one of the benches and absorb the atmosphere.

9 Turn left to retrace your steps along Akeman Street and Mere Way, passing the farms, this time, on your right-hand side. The metalled road gives way to the bridleway and passes Sunclose Farm on the left. Continue until you reach Butt Lane, where you cross the road and turn left, then take the path back to the starting point at the Milton Park and Ride.

⧖ walk sixteen

A Wandlebury Wander

A country estate and an Iron Age hill fort.

Cambridge is very flat. It has street signs for Peas Hill, Market Hill and Senate House Hill, but they are all flat! These places are just a few metres above sea level. But a couple of miles from the southeastern edge of the city lie the Gog Magog Hills, where two legendary Iceni giants were said to live. These hills are the home of Wandlebury Country Park.

This circular walk takes you through the park's beautiful woods and alongside chalk meadows. It begins around the perimeter of an 18th-century estate, with vistas of Cambridge and across to Ely. The second part of the walk goes along the bottom of a defensive ring, the remains of an Iron Age hill fort. Trees meet overhead, and dappled light freckles the ground. You will feel like you are walking inside a hidden green tunnel; children will particularly enjoy it.

Leaving the ring through an orchard and walled garden, the walk ends at a grand Grade II listed stable block, topped by a fine cupola clock tower. Discover the grave of the famous racehorse, Godolphin Arabian, the subject of American children's writer Marguerite Henry's book, *King of the Wind*. The park is run by Cambridge Past Present and Future, an independent charity who protect the ancient history and manage the land's flora and fauna to promote its biodiversity.

start / finish	Wandlebury Country Park car park, Wandlebury Ring, off Babraham Road
nearest postcode	CB22 3AE
distance	2¼ miles / 3.5 km
time	1 hour
terrain	Surfaced and dirt paths, which can be muddy. Steep slopes and possibility of fallen branches.

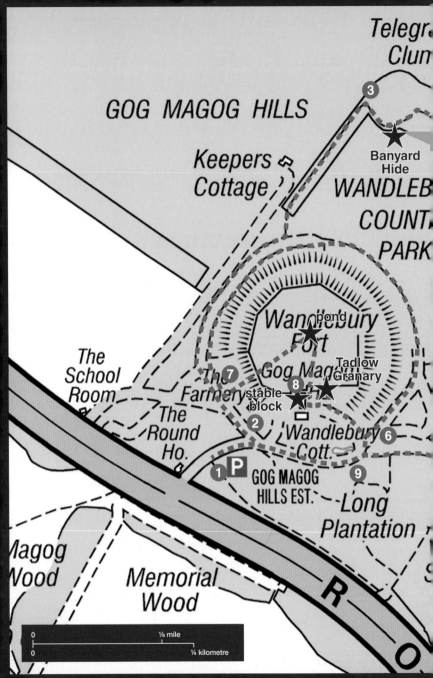

Ely
Viewpoint

Green
Ride

Round
Clump

Roman R

Lodge

Long
Plantation

Furze
Clump

ol
et

Wormwood
Hill

1 At the car park information board, take the first path on the left. A fingerpost points to Trevelyan Gate, Banyard Hide and Ely Viewpoint. The first part of the walk is clearly signed. Take the first right, and bear right. The route goes through woods, with an Iron Age ring on the right side.

2 Turn left, away from the Ring, and keep following signs to Ely Viewpoint. The path is wide and easy to navigate. In spring, there are cowslips and in the autumn, a carpet of cobnuts. There are little breaks in the trees where you get lovely views over the fields towards Cambridge. On the right, there are fields which may have Highland cattle grazing. Continue with a handsome row of beech trees on your left.

3 At the corner of the field, bear right. Continue alongside a meadow on the right. You could stop at Banyard Hide ★ to look at some of the many woodland and farmland birds. There are coppiced hazel trees, and stretches beside the path are sown with native arable wild flower seeds to attract bees and butterflies. Continue to Ely Viewpoint ★. Benches are plentiful where you can stop and enjoy the surroundings.

4 At the Ely Viewpoint, turn right following the sign to the Roman Road and Emma's Gate. Go past a meadow on the right, and back into the woods. Turn right at a signpost to the Car Park and Inner Ring. On both sides there are hedges with meadows and chalky downland beyond; you may see red kites or buzzards.

5 Turn right at the Games Field and walk up the hill to a hard surfaced track with low bollards along the edge. Turn right. The road curves round to a little bridge. Don't cross the bridge, but take a small, chalk path to the right just before the bridge starts. Go down a steep slope into the ring – the remains of an Iron Age fortification ditch.

6 Don't go under the bridge; walk away from it, along the bottom of the ring. Follow this natural tunnel, with leaves underfoot and overhead. Pass a kissing gate on the left, which leads through to a walled garden (which you will explore later). There is an interesting display board with pictures and information about the Ring's history. Continue along the ditch as you circle about three-quarters of the way around the Ring. This is a magical path for children to explore, with fallen trees and the ditch walls to climb.

7 The Ring has a small break where it has been filled in with earth. At this point, climb up to ground level, and turn left into an orchard. Go straight ahead, through a door into a walled garden. Walk diagonally left across a large expanse of grass to visit a pond ★ and look at the water wildlife. Then turn and walk towards the stable block ★ , which looks more like a grand house, with its fine cupola and clock tower.

8 When you reach the stables, walk through the archway. There are toilets on the left. The stalls that were built for racehorses have now been converted into homes – visitors are allowed to look around but asked to be respectful of the residents. The grave of the racehorse Godolphin Arabian is under the archway. Turn left beyond this, walk through the courtyard, and on to Tadlow Granary ★ . The granary is raised off the ground – this was to stop rats eating the corn. There may be a pop-up café at this spot. Behind it is an outbuilding used for education. Carry on to return to the main track, with bollards along each side, and cross the small bridge.

9 Bear right and pass another pond on the right. The track ends back at the car park.

ᴀᴢ walk seventeen

Wool Street

Hildersham, Linton and a Roman road.

The villages of Hildersham and Linton are both ancient villages, mentioned in the Domesday Book of 1086. This country walk starts in Hildersham, 8 miles (13 km) to the southeast of Cambridge. This ancient village is situated on a tributary of the River Cam, known locally as the River Granta, which you cross as you leave the village. A footpath across arable farmland will take you to a Roman road running along the chalk ridge. Records refer to this as Wool Street, suggesting that traders in wool once used this road. Look out for wild flowers and butterflies, and birds singing in the hedgerows and soaring overhead.

Rivey Lane leads you across farmland and past the Chilford Hall Vineyard, one of the oldest established vineyards in England. You will pass the Rivey Water Tower, a striking example of Art Deco design and a prominent landmark for miles around, as you climb Rivey Hill, which overlooks the village of Linton. At 367 feet (112 m), it is the highest point for several miles – a good place to stop a while to take in the views.

This walk is a mix of hills and wetlands, with the route descending to Linton along a bridleway and returning to the start along the valley of the River Granta.

There is a bus service from Cambridge to Hildersham High Street and on-street parking is available.

start / finish	Pear Tree Inn, High Street, Hildersham
nearest postcode	CB21 6BU
distance	6½ miles / 10.5 km
time	3 hours 30 minutes
terrain	Pavements and paved walkways. Grass verges and paths. Footpaths and bridleways which can be muddy. Steep slope.

❶ Begin the walk in the centre of the village of Hildersham, with your back to the Pear Tree Inn. Turn left to head north up the High Street, towards the white painted bridge where the road crosses the River Granta. The River Granta is a tributary of the River Cam which flows through Cambridge. After leaving Cambridge, the Cam joins the River Great Ouse which eventually drains into the North Sea. Pass Holy Trinity Church ★ , with its 12th-century tower, on the left. The church is constructed from flint and rubble as stone and brick were uncommon in this part of East Anglia. The pavement ends as you leave the village, so care is needed where the grass verge isn't wide enough to walk on.

❷ At the crossroads junction with Hildersham Road, cross straight over. Hildersham Road leads from the village of Abingdon to Linton, and the road ahead is Balsham Road, where you are heading.

❸ After a third of a mile (400 metres), the hedgerow on the left ends and there is a public footpath leading across farmland towards a small wooded area on the distant ridge ahead. Take this path and continue for three-quarters of a mile (1.3 km) until you reach a gateway across the footpath.

❹ Turn right onto a narrow track. This is the old Roman road that linked Colchester (at one time the capital of Roman Britain) with Godmanchester, another important town and fort. Where this road crossed the River Cam, a small Roman town grew, later to become Cambridge. After about a mile (1.5 km) the Roman road is intersected by the road that leads back into Hildersham, but cross this and follow the Roman road straight ahead for a further mile (1.5 km). You might find blackberries or sloe berries along the way depending on the season.

❺ At the next road junction leave the Roman road, turn right onto the B1052 and follow this towards the water tower that is visible ahead. Take care to keep to the right on this road, walking towards the oncoming traffic; there is no footpath but there is a grass verge beside the road. Continue past the Chilford Hall Vineyard ★ . Vines were first planted here in 1972 and all the wines produced are made exclusively from the grapes grown and harvested here.

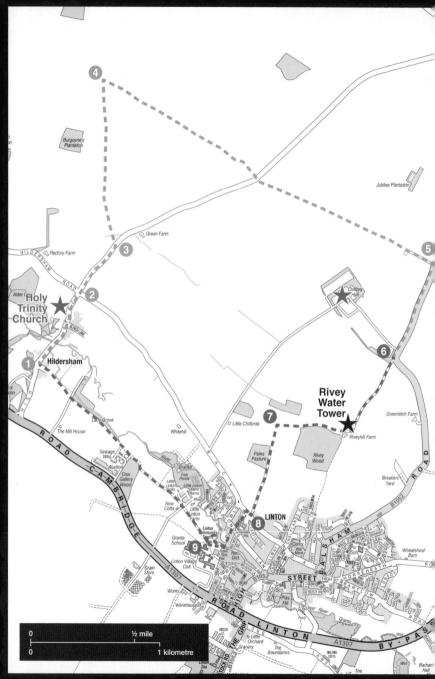

Holy Trinity Church

Hildersham

Rivey Water Tower

LINTON

Burgoyne's Plantation

Jubilee Plantation

HILDERSHAM ROAD

Rectory Farm

Green Farm

Chilford Hall

Alder Carr

BENDS LANE

Greenditch Farm

Riveyhill Farm

Little Chilfords

Whitehill

Pains Pasture

Rivey Wood

Breakers Yard

Lady Grove

The Mill House

River Granta

Sewage Wks.

Abattoir

Cow Gallery Wood

Little Linton Mill

Fish Ponds

Little Linton Farm

Moat

New Colts

Little Linton Farm

Linton Community

Granta School

Linton Village Coll.

Grain Store

Works

Warehouses

Wheatsheaf Barn

HIGH STREET

BALSHAM ROAD

B1052

CAMBRIDGE ROAD

A1307

LINTON BY-PASS

A1307

THE GRIP

Play Fld.

Ford

Weir

River Granta

Malting Cotts

The Boundaries

Barham Hall

BARTLOW ROAD

B1053

HORSEHEATH ROAD

❶ ❷ ❸ ❹ ❺ ❻ ❼ ❽ ❾

0 ½ mile
0 1 kilometre

6 As the road bends to the left, take the wide driveway straight ahead towards the Rivey Water Tower ★. This was built in 1936 and supplied Linton with its first mains water. The driveway bends round to the right after the water tower, past private houses and between paddocks. Follow this driveway along the ridge behind ancient woodland. Keep to the footpath and the woodland will open out into farmland with wonderful views of the village of Linton and beyond. Perhaps take the opportunity to pause and enjoy a picnic!

7 The footpath turns left to continue down the hill and emerges in the village. The path is quite steep and can be muddy. Linton is an ancient village, mentioned in the Domesday Book. It is situated on the Icknield Way path, a 110-mile (177-km) route from Ivinghoe Beacon in Buckinghamshire to the start of the Peddars Way in Suffolk, which is popular with walkers, horse riders and off-road cyclists.

8 Cross the street, turning right and then left onto Crabtree Croft which leads to a footpath past some houses. Cross Symonds Lane, continuing on the footpath. When you reach the recreation ground, turn right onto the footpath skirting the children's play area, or if dry underfoot cut across the play area, heading to the corner diagonally to the right. Go through the gate in the corner and emerge immediately into a fenced path across a field between paddocks where horses often graze.

9 Follow this path straight ahead for just over a mile (1.5 km), crossing Little Linton, and then running parallel to the valley of the River Granta, passing paddocks, a water treatment plant, farm buildings and gardens. The River Granta is a chalk stream; its valley is an ancient trackway and an interesting wetland habitat with many birds and wild flowers. The path joins the end of the road called Meadowlands, joining High Street, and leads back to the centre of Hildersham village.

ᴀz walk eighteen

St Ives Circle

The market town on the river.

This walk begins at the old sheep market in St Ives, a pretty market town 12 miles (19 km) northwest of Cambridge, sitting on the banks of the River Great Ouse. From medieval times it was an important port. The first part of the walk is along the main thoroughfare, with its fine statue to local lad, OliverCromwell. It also passes the delightful Norris Museum with its extensive local history collection.

There is much to enjoy on this route, which goes out along the river to Houghton Mill, built in 1754. An earlier mill was recorded in the Domesday Book. The walk takes you through woodland and water meadows, with many willows and expansive views of field and skyscape. You will cross the river and its floodplain before circling back to St Ives. High spots include the gardens of Hemingford Manor (look out for the slightly hidden gate to this magical place, enshrined in the children's story books of Lucy Boston). Also the magnificent St James' Church on the riverbank at Hemingford Grey.

The walk ends by crossing a six-arched medieval bridge, with its sailors' chapel jutting out into the river. This is one of only four such buildings in the country. There are plenty of options for a good tea or pub lunch after your walk.

There is a guided bus service to St Ives, from Cambridge railway station and the city centre.

start / finish	Bus station, Market Street, St Ives
nearest postcode	PE27 5AH
distance	6 miles / 9.5 km
time	3 hours
terrain	Paved roads. Footpaths which may be muddy. Kissing gates.

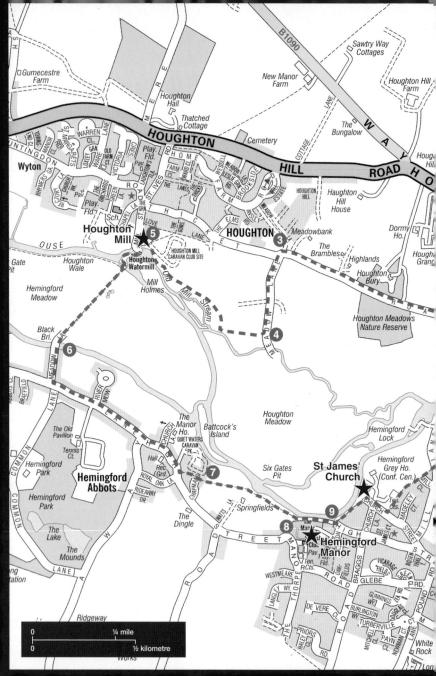

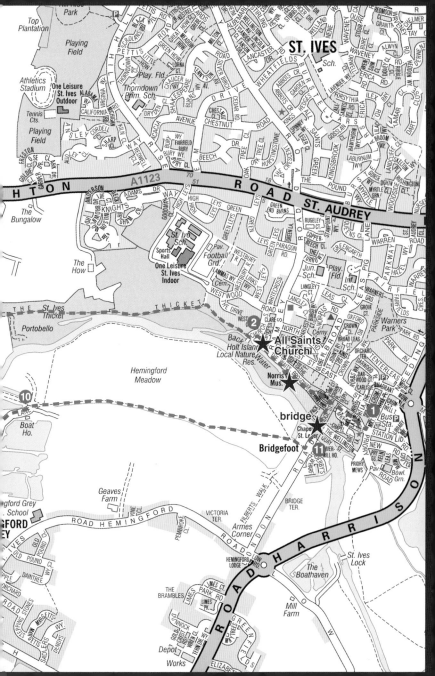

1 Starting at the bus station, turn left onto Market Road and right to Market Hill. Walk along this main thoroughfare of St Ives, following The Pavement, with its statue of Oliver Cromwell, Crown Street and The Broadway. At the Norris Museum ★ , head to the left to walk beside the river to All Saints Church ★ . Look at the carvings on the West door where you will find a rabbit nipping down a hole on the top right, and another popping out on the left.

2 Leave the churchyard at the back of the church and pass a white bridge to Holt Island Nature Reserve on your left. Keeping to the left of the wall, follow signs for Ouse Valley Way and go west along Barnes Walk, a leafy metalled path, with views of the river. The path takes you through a wooded area called The Thicket and goes past the Copley Scouting Centre.

3 Just over a mile (1.9 km) after the Scouting Centre, the path becomes a road and another path joins from the right. At this junction, take the path on your left. There is a wide gate across the entrance, but pedestrians can walk through a gap just beyond the gate. Continue along the wide, straight path for a short distance. There are fields on either side – you may see llamas in one of them.

4 At a sign saying 'New Public Footpath', turn right. This path is narrower and less straight than the previous ones. Go past a little bridge on the left, then cross a small wooden bridge (over a ditch which may be dry). Go through a kissing gate, on the left, to National Trust's Waterclose Meadow. There is a pleasant, wooded area before you reach a wide mill pond.

5 Then the magnificent Houghton Mill ★ rises up above the river. It was built in 1754 and is now run by the National Trust (check opening times). Flour is still ground here, and as well as the mill workings, there is a room set up to remember the time when the building served as a Youth Hostel. Toilets and a café are available. Walk under the mill and across a weir. This is a good place to pause and look for the many water birds which thrive along this river plain. There are interesting information boards at this point. The path curves round to a water meadow. Take the very straight path which goes across it, until you reach a bridge over another branch of the river.

6 Cross the bridge and walk along Meadow Lane into Hemingford Abbots. Turn left into Common Lane and the High Street with their pretty thatched cottages and a charming old schoolhouse. Pass the Axe and Compass pub on the left, and after Manor Lane, take the footpath to the left. It's a narrow path, to the side of a house, with fences on each side and is signed to the Great Ouse and Hemingford Grey.

7 At the end of the lane, go through a kissing gate. Take the path directly across a field. Go through another gate and bear right. There are several more gates before an expansive view of the Ouse is revealed. Continue along a raised riverbank, lined with willows – a favourite perch for kingfishers. Pause to enjoy the big East Anglian sky.

8 The path draws towards houses and moored boats. Look out on the right for the rather hidden back gate to Hemingford Manor ★ , the oldest inhabited house in England. It was built in Norman times and was more recently home to Lucy Boston, author of the Green Knowe children's books. There is a charge to enter and visit the wonderful topiary gardens. It may be possible to arrange tours of the house on prior application.

9 At a road, keep left along the river to St James' Church ★ , with its Norman arch dating from 1186. Sand martins nest in holes in the walls. There is a moving memorial on the chancel floor to two little girls who may have died of the plague. On exiting the church, turn left and walk along Church Street. Turn left along Love Lane, signed back to St Ives. Join Meadow Lane and follow signs to Hemingford Meadow.

10 At the end of Meadow Lane, a kissing gate, on the left, opens onto a large water meadow, with the spires of two St Ives churches in the distance. The footpath runs along the right side of the field, parallel to the path taken on the outward journey on the other side of the river. As you near St Ives, the path swings diagonally to the left. Go under an archway through hotel grounds.

11 Turn left onto London Road to re-enter the town. Cross the beautiful old bridge ★ . In the middle is a tiny chapel, one of only four in the country built for sailors loading and unloading goods. You may want to pause on The Quay, where boats are moored and ducks fed. There are benches and tea shops and a fine view of the bridge and its chapel, jutting into the river. To finish, go along Bridge Street, turn right along Crown Street and left up Market Road to return to the bus station.

🄰🄯 walk nineteen

The Isle of Eels

The River Great Ouse at Ely.

Ely was once an island, accessible only by boat in the undrained, swampy fen landscape. The first Christian community was founded here in the 7th century by Etheldreda, the daughter of the King of East Anglia, and today the hilltop is dominated by the Norman cathedral, known as 'the ship of the fens'.

The river has always played an important role in the city's history. The Ely monks were some of the main river traders and would travel by river to Cambridge, where they founded colleges. Eels were a major source of food and income here for centuries. Ely's last commercial eel catcher retired in 2016, and the city holds an annual Eel Festival which celebrates its past as 'The Isle of Eels'.

This walk takes you past houseboats, inns, old maltings, the island of Babylon, tranquil green spaces and views over the Fens. You will discover Roswell Pitts – originally excavated to provide clay for constructing flood banks along nearby fenland rivers, now a haven for wildlife and fishermen. Return via the country park with a stunning view of Ely Cathedral, passing some of the city's quaintest houses and discovering Jubilee Gardens with their secretive eel – just about to make a break for the river.

Ely lies 24 miles (38 km) northeast of the centre of Cambridge and can be reached by train or bus from the city. There are several free car parks.

start / finish	Ely Railway Station, Station Road, Ely
nearest postcode	CB7 4BS
distance	3½ miles / 5.5 km
time	1 hour 30 minutes
terrain	Paved and gravel roads and paths. Dirt paths which may be muddy. Kissing gates and slopes.

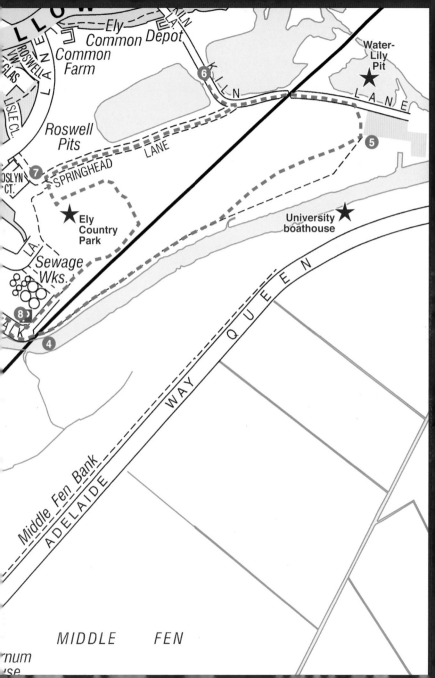

❶ From the railway station turn right onto Bridge Road and walk along the pavement under the bridge, then cross over this road and also the slip road leading to the marina and a disused level crossing. Turn right along the pavement. Just before the bridge over the river, you come to a footpath on the left, which slopes down to the River Great Ouse.

❷ Take this path and continue past houseboats and boatyards and then follow the river path as it curves round to the right in front of The Cutter Inn ★ – named after the workmen who lodged here whilst 'cutting' a new channel for the river. Continue along the riverside with the Island of Babylon on your right. Once home to 40 households, this is now a large marina. Continue past a riverside bar and then houses on the left.

❸ At the road bridge leading to the island, continue along the river with the Babylon Gallery on the left. Follow the path lined with willows until it passes under a railway bridge, through a kissing gate and into the open countryside.

❹ The field here sometimes contains cows but they are well acclimatized to people and dogs. The gravel path takes you to the end of the field, and there are opportunities to take grassy paths on the right to stay close to the river, if wished. A sign on the left of the path about halfway along indicates the flood meadows which are important breeding and wintering sites for birds. At the end of the field, the modern building on the far side of the river is the boathouse for Cambridge University ★. The rowers train here, rather than in Cambridge, as there is a large uncongested stretch of water. The annual Oxford-Cambridge Boat Race has taken place here twice in its history.

❺ The path turns left through another kissing gate, up past some industrial buildings on the right to Kiln Lane. In front of you is the Water-Lily Pit ★, another important area for wildlife. Turn left onto the lane and continue over the level crossing. At the end of the layby on the left is another kissing gate which you will pass through, but before doing so a short diversion along the road will take you past views of Roswell Pits, with the sailing club at the far end on the right. Continue round the right-hand bend and you soon come to another lake on the left with a fabulous view of the cathedral beyond.

6 Retrace your steps to the kissing gate at the layby, pass through it and continue along the path between the trees.

7 Just before the path turns right, turn left up a wooden ramp into Ely Country Park ★. Take the resin path on the left and follow it round to the right until you see a large play area in the next field. Leave the path and continue straight on under the trees and up the grassy incline at the end. This turns right and leads to a lookout bench with views over the railway line, river and fens. Continue on as the path descends, then turns left and joins the resin path which in turn leads through a car parking area.

8 At the end of the car park, turn right onto Willow Walk and follow it round to the left, passing a children's playground on your right. Continue left onto Waterside and on towards the river. There are some interesting old houses and buildings in this area, including Waterside Antiques in an old granary.

9 Turn right here and retrace your steps along the river, past The Maltings – once used to malt barley and now a theatre, restaurant and bar – and on to an open area on your right called Jubilee Gardens. This was once a hive of industry for the port area, containing holding fishponds, tanneries, breweries and potteries. Nowadays you can stroll round the gardens, look at the giant metal eel sculpture and try to discover the mosaic eel made from thousands of pieces of ancient pottery, found here when the area was excavated.

10 Head back down to the river and turn right past The Cutter Inn. Originally there was no path here – the pub was right on the riverbank and there were many incidents of people leaving the pub and falling in the river. In 1906 a local man, James Merry, who lived on Babylon, was presented with a medal by the council for saving 21 men from drowning. Leave the river and continue straight ahead along Annesdale, until you come to Station Road. Turn left here, cross over at the pedestrian crossing, walk left, and you'll come to the railway station.

▲Z walk twenty

Ely City

The cathedral and Cromwell's House.

Ely, one of England's smallest cities, boasts a rich and diverse history. Hereward the Wake is said to have provided the final opposition to the Norman Conquest here in this once fenland island refuge, the event which ultimately gave the city its stunning cathedral.

Discover the only surviving house of Ely's most famous resident, Oliver Cromwell, and learn why there is a Russian canon on Palace Green, before taking in the imposing west front of the cathedral. Explore the large complex of monastic buildings, and view the Lady Chapel and Octagon tower as you walk around the cathedral precincts. This walk takes in the small city centre, including the option to visit the newly refurbished museum with its Anglo-Saxon treasure, before heading down to the tranquil riverside with antique shops, many boats and resident wildlife. Look out for a yellow giraffe on your way!

You will see signs of eels, which are said to have given Ely its name, as you return via gardens and parks with yet more views of the cathedral. Don't miss the medieval cottages in Silver Street and the Thomas Parsons' Almshouses, built on the site of the former Tithe Barn.

Ely lies 24 miles (38 km) northeast of the centre of Cambridge and can be reached by train or bus from the city. There are several free car parks.

start / finish	Ely Tourist Information Office, St Mary's Street, Ely
nearest postcode	CB7 4HF
distance	2¼ miles / 3.7 km
time	1 hour
terrain	Paved roads and walkways. Some slopes.

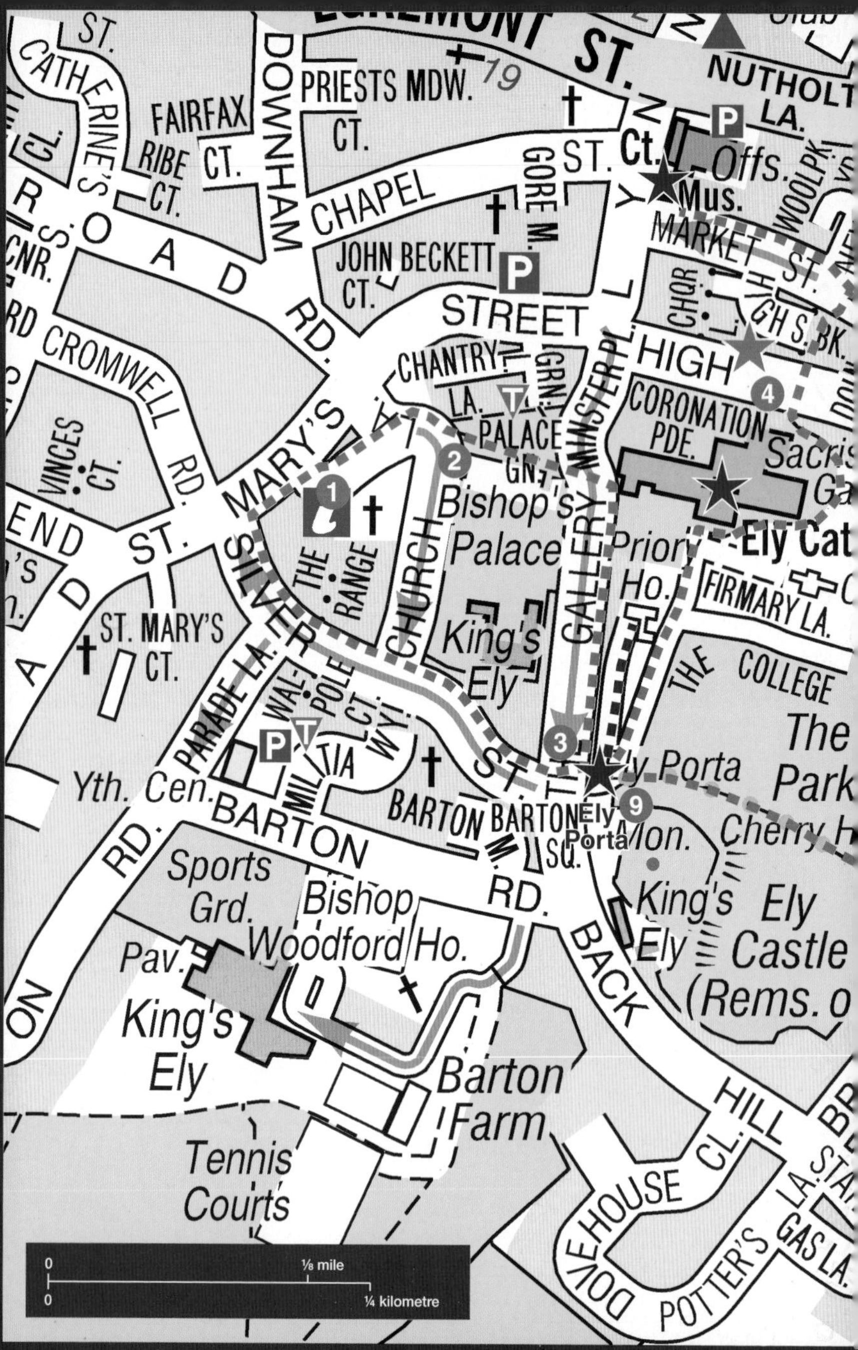

EGREMONT ST.

NUTHOLT LA.

ST. CATHERINE'S

CNR.

ROAD

FAIRFAX RIBE CT.

DOWNHAM RD.

PRIESTS MDW. CT.

CHAPEL

JOHN BECKETT CT.

GORE M.

ST.

Ct.

Offs.

Mus.

MARKET ST.

WOOLPK.

CHANTRY LA.

STREET

PALACE GN.

CROMWELL RD.

VINCES CT.

END

ST.

ST. MARY'S CT.

MARY'S

SILVER

PARADE LA.

THE RANGE

CHURCH

Bishop's Palace

King's Ely

CHOR.

HIGH

CORONATION PDE.

GH S. BK.

Sacris Ga

Ely Cat

Priory Ho.

FIRMARY LA.

GALLERY

MINSTER PL.

GRN.

ST.

Ely Porta

Ely Porta Ion.

THE

COLLEGE

The Park

Cherry H

WALPOLE LCT. WY.

MILITIA

Yth. Cen.

BARTON

RD.

Sports Grd.

Pav.

King's Ely

Bishop Woodford Ho.

BARTON

BARTON SQ.

BACK

King's Ely Castle (Rems. o

HILL

Barton Farm

Tennis Courts

DOVEHOUSE

POTTER'S LA.

GAS LA.

STA.

0 ⅛ mile
0 ¼ kilometre

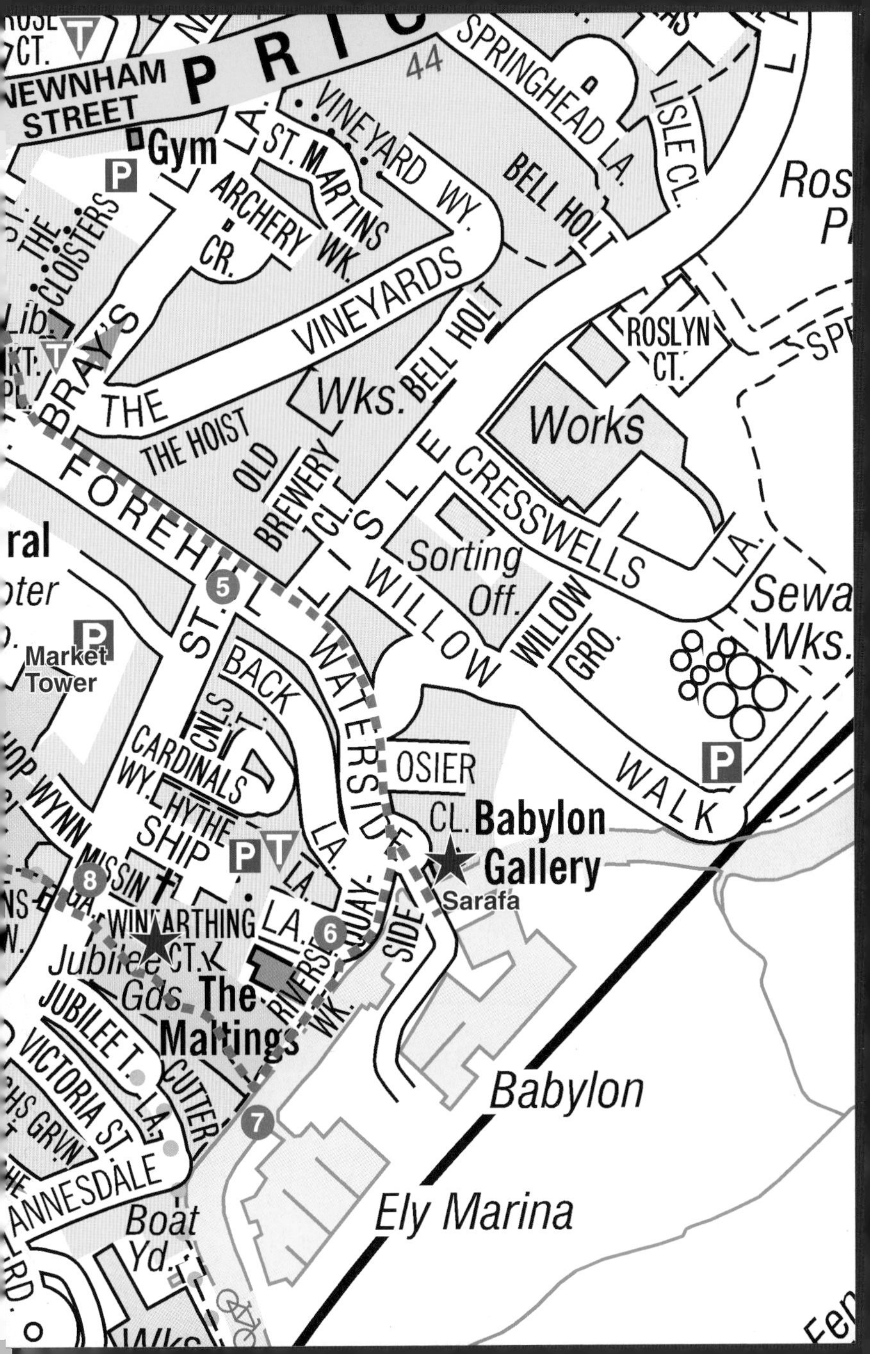

NEWNHAM STREET

PRIORY

44

SPRINGHEAD LA.

LISLE CL.

Ros
P

Gym

ST. MARTINS WK.

VINEYARD WY.

BELL HOLT

ARCHERY CR.

THE CLOISTERS

ROSLYN CT.

Lib.

BRAY'S

THE VINEYARDS

THE HOIST

Wks.

BELL HOLT

Works

OLD BREWERY CL.

FOREH

THE

LISLE

CRESSWELLS LA.

Sorting Off.

ral

Market Tower

ST. K

BACK

CNLS. T.

WILLOW

WILLOW GRO.

Sewa Wks.

5

WATERSI

CARDINALS WY.

HYTHE

OSIER CL.

Babylon Gallery

WALK

SHIP

T.

LA.

QUAY-SIDE

Sarafa

WYNN

MISSIN

8

WINARTHING CT.

T.

LA.

6

RIVERS WK.

Jubilee Gds

The Maltings

JUBILEE T.

LA.

7

Babylon

VICTORIA ST

CUTTER

CHS GRVN.

Boat Yd.

ANNESDALE

Ely Marina

Wks.

1 With your back to the Tourist Information Office/Oliver Cromwell's House, turn slightly to the right and head in the direction of the cathedral, passing the Old Fire Engine House on the left where once two fire engines were kept, but is now used as a restaurant. St Mary's Church, to the right, was where one of Oliver Cromwell's daughters was baptized and contains a plaque commemorating the five Littleport rioters, who were hung in June 1816.

2 Continue across Palace Green, not forgetting to look at the canon, a relic of the Crimean War, given by Queen Victoria in 1860, to the towering West front of the cathedral ★ . Turn right along The Gallery with the old Bishop's Palace on the right and new Bishop's Palace, followed by monastic buildings, on the left.

3 At the mini-roundabout turn left under the 14th-century Porta gate ★ , once a main entrance into the monastic precincts. Make a short detour at this point along the path immediately on the left to view more of the monastic buildings and Prior Crauden's Chapel. Retrace your steps and follow the road around to the left. You might want to look along Firmary Lane on the right, once the main hall of the aisled monastic infirmary built in the 12th century, before continuing around the east side of the cathedral noting the Lady Chapel and Octagon Tower.

4 Leave the cathedral precincts by the Sacrists gate and cross the High Street, going into High Street Passage, with its gift shops and then on to Market Street. Another detour, turning left along Market Street, brings you to Ely Museum ★ (entry fee), once the old Gaol House, found on the right at the junction with Lynn Road. Turn back along Market Street, which takes you on to Market Place. Its Corn Exchange and Town Hall have long since been demolished. Walk diagonally across to continue your walk down Fore Hill.

5 Where Fore Hill bends to the right, continue straight ahead into Waterside with its antiques barn, once an old granary, and a variety of interesting houses and buildings, displaying signs of a more prosperous past. It is worth taking a few steps onto Babylon Bridge, leading to the marina, for attractive views along the river from both sides. Look out for a yellow giraffe, called Sarafa ★ , who might just be sticking her neck up above the rooftops!